Helping Kids Heal

75 Activities to Help Children Recover
from Trauma and Loss

Rebecca Carman, CSW

ISBN 10: # 1-56688-723-2

ISBN 13: 978-1-56688-723-6

Published and distributed by:

THE BUREAU®
FOR AT-RISK YOUTH
Promoting Growth Through Knowledge
A Brand of The Guidance Group
1-800-99-YOUTH
www.guidance-group.com

Acknowledgements

Special thanks to my readers Kendall Johnson, Ph.D. and Stanley Goldklang, Ph.D. for delivering invaluable feedback at record speed.

I also want to thank Griffen Jack, the relief and development agency Mercy Corps, and all the many others who helped bring Comfort for Kids to life. Mercy Corps created Comfort for Kids—an innovative training program—in partnership with JPMorgan Chase, Bright Horizons and the Dougy Center after the World Trade Center disaster.

Thanks to my husband Nicholas Dawidoff who provided support throughout and key background information for the activity on page 101.

And finally, heartfelt appreciation to Sally Germain at The Bureau for At-Risk Youth for championing *Helping Kids Heal* from beginning to end.

Please contact me at RWCarman@aol.com with any comments or questions. I welcome feedback and the submission of new activities for the next edition of *Helping Kids Heal*.

TABLE OF CONTENTS

Section 1. Establishing Safety

These activities are designed to help children feel safe—in their thoughts and bodies, in their immediate surroundings, with therapists themselves. Therapists can assist children as they regain their footing: "The traumatic event is over; together, we occupy a benign here-and-now." Like sandbags by water's edge, these activities are our first defense in safeguarding the child from overwhelming affect. Since children need to connect with their therapists, several activities are also included toward this end.

Section 2. Easing into Relaxation

These activities help children cope with tension and stress, and can be used to deescalate emotions if they spiral out of control. Before children do the "work" of therapy, they need to find ways to modulate the intense physiological reactions that may arise. Reestablishing safety and the ability to let down one's guard are prerequisites for treatment, and paradoxically, the end result. Let these activities assume the familiar quality of ritual, and return to them again and again during the child's healing process.

Section 3. Learning about Feelings

These activities help children identify and understand various emotions. Reading and interpreting emotions is like a language unto itself; we therapists can serve as translators as children sort out feelings in themselves and others. In addition, we can introduce the notion that children's emotions and reactions make perfect sense, given what they have experienced. The ability to understand feelings is vital when maneuvering through painful emotional terrain.

TABLE OF CONTENTS

Section 4. Stuck and Unstuck

Throughout the world, people sing, dance and move as a way of transcending trauma. These are physical exercises to help emotions flow through children's bodies and be released. As we all know, children would rather cavort than talk about feelings. These activities build on the vocabulary of emotions and are reassuring to kids: Maybe therapy won't be so bad after all.

Section 5. What Actually Happened

These activities help ensure that the child has a baseline understanding of the traumatic event. They check the child's knowledge of the facts, and address distortions and confusion potentially impeding recovery and peace of mind. During these activities and those in the next section, be sure to monitor the intensity of children's reactions and make a transition if need be. Plan your "exit strategy" ahead of time with activities stressing safety, relaxation, or empowerment.

Section 6. Expressing Feelings

These activities support children as they revisit the event and the accompanying feelings; without taking this risk, the child will be unable to truly move forward. "You have to go through the bad parts to get to the other side"—this oft-repeated wisdom is the underpinning of this section. Expressing scary, overwhelming, and dark emotions in the presence of a compassionate other is central to the process of healing. It's no easy task to tolerate the pain of children's experiences, but this witnessing is so important. This time the child is not alone.

TABLE OF CONTENTS

Section 7. Taming the Dragon

Traumatic events leave a litany of negative emotions in their wake, from anxiety to anger to apathy. These activities are designed to help children cope with unpleasant and self-destructive feelings, paving the way for feeling better. Intended to go hand-in-hand with those in "Expressing Feelings," these activities assist children as they regain control of their bodies and emotions. Slowly, children can begin to integrate the distress of what has happened to them.

Section 8. Cherishing Memories

Because traumatic events may include the death of a loved one, these activities support children as they grieve. The activities in this section are designed to help children reckon with loss, hold on to memories, and internalize sources of validation and strength.

Section 9. Restoring Balance and Trust

These activities promote a sense of stability and benevolence in the world. Whereas "Taming the Dragon" addresses threats emanating from the inside—feeling states associated with PTSD, for example—this section helps children withstand real-life stress. Intended to fortify, center and protect, these activities encourage children to venture back into the rough-and-tumble world.

TABLE OF CONTENTS

Section 10. I Can Feel Good

These activities address children's self-esteem. Especially in cases of abuse and neglect, children feel devalued by others and thus never learn to nurture themselves. By practicing constructive internal talk, recognizing strengths, and gaining perspective about what transpired, children can begin to appreciate their talents and goodness.

Section 11. Heroes

Heroes overcome difficult circumstances to reach goals they never dreamed possible. These activities reinforce children's growing sense of self-efficacy and power, while acknowledging that some negative feelings and scenarios never quite go away. Here, we celebrate the courage necessary for emotional growth, and the arc of the hero's journey from despair to a sense of optimism and well-being.

Section 12. Wishes and Dreams

"Trauma is a disorder of the imagination," says one expert, referring to the tendency to get "stuck" and visualize solely what one has experienced. These activities foster children's creative and imaginative life, including the ability to contemplate fundamentally different futures. We end with activities about making dreams come true.

TABLE OF CONTENTS

Section 13. Growing and Giving Back

These activities cultivate children's compassion and empathy. After a traumatic event, survivors must consciously choose to break the cycle; without active support, hurtful attitudes may be perpetuated. For many children, helping others is healing in and of itself.

Introduction

The Yanomamo tribe in Brazil practices the ultimate activity to help kids heal. When something bad happens to a child—say, a boy tumbles off a steep cliff—all the women and children in the village gather round. After physical wounds are tended to, hours are dedicated to that child's psychic recovery. One by one, villagers reenact the traumatic event for the child, pantomiming falling and landing, falling and landing, over and over again.

Gradually, the reenactment begins to change, becoming antic and fanciful, absent of pain. Perhaps child rescuers appear at just the right moment or green foliage miraculously cushions the fall. Mesmerized, the child watches this performance and his state of mind starts to shift. The villagers continue their dramatic play. The child starts smiling and then laughing, finally ceasing to be upset altogether.

We in the United States lack these kinds of communal rituals to cope with terrifying events. We generally look to priests or therapists to help recover meaning and emotional stability—often, strangers to the victim before catastrophe struck. Our culture's priorities leave us with little time or sense of community, yet therapists are expected to "put back the pieces" after children are exposed to ever more horrific acts.

Helping Kids Heal is written with you, the therapist who works with traumatized children, in mind. While we can't re-create the societal conditions of the Yanomamo under the florescent lights of our offices, we can draw from their wisdom and seek—through relationship, witnessing, and creative expression—to bring that spark back into a child's eyes. By using therapeutic attitudes and some serious play, therapists can "reset" a child's state of mind. The 75 activities that follow are designed to help you do just that.

This book is geared toward therapists working with children ages five through twelve. Most activities are suitable for individual work with children; several group activities are included as well. *Helping Kids Heal* contains thirteen sections, ordered to approximate the natural sequence of recovery. Thus, children move from relaxation exercises, to "reality testing" what has happened, to managing difficult emotions, to building a healthy sense of self-esteem, to achieving the capacity to give back to others. Because trauma so often involves loss, some grieving activities are included as well. Regardless of the specifics of what has happened, these activities are effective in helping children heal.

The ideas to follow come from my own work as a psychotherapist with children, interviews with practitioners, a review of contributions to the literature, and most importantly, the healing of children that took place after the World Trade Center disaster. As Program Manager for Mercy Corps' Comfort for Kids (a trauma education program that trained nearly 7,000 participants from New York City's at-risk communities), I was privy to innumerable stories from the field. I have been extraordinarily moved by the creativity and dedication of these caregivers, and have them to thank for the heart and soul of this book.

I trust you'll enjoy these activities as much as I have enjoyed collecting them. From rolling snakes, to painting masks, to building paper towel tube bridges, to monster management, to makin' rain, to zooming rockets, these activities entice even the most exhausted children and adults to kick up their heels. Please let me know what you think—I'd love to hear which activities you found most effective and suggestions for new ones I should include next time around.

I was working with a six-year-old girl a few years ago, and she spontaneously started writing a book of "advice" for her younger sister (the basis for the activity "Guru of the Future," pg. 110). This skittish, brown-eyed child showed me something profound in that instant, the urge to transform knowledge of pain into something of benefit to another. You may be adept at this art already. May you successfully transmit this gift to a child someday!

A Special Note from the Author

If you've sought out this book, you likely know a child who has experienced some sort of traumatic event. This event could be a natural disaster like a flood or hurricane, or a distinctly human act such as terrorism or battery at the hands of a relative. With luck, this was an isolated incident in the child's life. But all too often, therapists work with children who have known little nurturing or joy, and are trying heroically to make sense of the apparently indifferent world around them.

During all our Comfort for Kids trainings, countless participants spoke of the high levels of violence endemic to their communities. Adrienne, a Social Worker from Harlem, summed it up this way: "Our children have a personal, ongoing experience of violence—from the gangs, to the drug use, to the fighting between parents. 9/11 just exacerbated what was already there, and with the economic downturn I see it getting worse. Kids are depressed, unmotivated for school, really angry… They are afraid to venture out and live their lives."

When I contemplate the reality of these children's lives, it's hard to imagine that a mere "activity" could make a difference. Why bother to draw "what your eyes might like to see" (Wonders of the World, pg. 103) when outside there's only concrete and blown-around litter? It's important to remember that these activities are not an end in and of themselves. They are meant to provide a "portal in" for caregivers—a way to open up conversation, to convey caring, to build trust and understanding, to imagine together other, more desirable realities. Like seeds in a packet, activities remain dormant until a caring adult breathes into them life and meaning.

———•———

What else is important to know about these activities, and play therapy in general? Here are some principles to bear in mind:

• Let children show you how they most prefer to communicate. Provide media that allow for symbolic expression, so painful terrain can be traversed indirectly and through metaphor.

• Create an atmosphere of acceptance. It's important not to make assumptions about what the child is thinking or feeling, or to take a judgmental or overly directive stance. As our Comfort for Kids mantra goes, "Listen! Listen! And listen some more!"

• Take care of yourself. Treating traumatized children is incredibly draining. Make sure you have plenty of support of your own.

Effective treatment requires a controlled return to the memory of the traumatic event, a chance to talk it out, play it out, draw it out and pound it out, all the while learning about myriad associated feelings. The goal is integration—the ability to look one's past straight in the eye and cultivate a sense of self based on inner strength, worth and ingenuity. This is a highly delicate operation, and *Helping Kids Heal* does not pretend to take the place of rigorous training and years of practice. This book functions on the premise that readers have some foundation of clinical training. If this is not the case, please consider getting ongoing supervision from someone you enjoy and respect.

Tips for Treating Traumatized Children

Children, like adults, typically exhibit four kinds of responses after an upsetting event. These include: hypcrarousal (jumpiness and anxiety); reexperiencing the event (flashbacks and intrusive memories); dissociation (feeling numb or "unreal"); and avoidance (staying away from reminders of the event).
The activities in this book are designed to help children progress within each of these realms—and plenty of others. However, if you plunge in haphazardly, the outcome can be worse than doing nothing at all! To avoid retraumatization—harkening back the child's original terrified state—please consider the following pointers:

• Don't overwhelm the child. Be sensitive to children's cues in terms of pacing and upsetting material. Be alert for signs that the child is getting overstimulated or dissociating and slow down immediately if this happens.

• Choose activities based on how fragile or sturdy the child appears to be. For children exhibiting the agitation or numbness characteristic of acute stress, select exercises that promote stabilization and self-soothing.

• Don't be afraid to modify an activity in mid-stride, if it appears to be too much for the child. The general rule of thumb to accomplish this is retreat (for the time being) from highly affective, personal and sensory material, and reorientation toward abstract and intellectual pursuits.

• When working with groups of children, consider the overall health of the group. Are kids alienated from each other, highly symptomatic, or a world apart in terms of needs? If so, consider activities that promote group consolidation and harmony. Children can thus learn to support each other before beginning the painful work of recovery.

There's no question that significant progress can happen during the fifty-minute hour, shifting the way a child sees himself and his future. But therapy becomes all the more potent when the child experiences an increasingly safe and nurturing family and community. The vital importance of empowering a child's caregivers cannot be overstated. Therapy that takes place in a vacuum—or worse yet, while emotional damage is still being inflicted—runs the risk of spinning in place. Anything you as a therapist can do to improve a child's external world will help that child exponentially.

As we all know, untreated trauma contributes to a litany of social ills as youth mature into young adults—from lost economic productivity, to health and mental health disorders, to drug and alcohol addiction, to criminal involvement. True healing leads to freedom, the ability to choose loving ways of being in the world instead of perpetuating what one has witnessed and received.

Nothing could be more important than your work on behalf of children. I hope *Helping Kids Heal* provides you with some measure of inspiration to carry forward.

ESTABLISHING SAFETY

These activities are designed to help children feel safe—in their thoughts and bodies, in their immediate surroundings, with therapists themselves. Therapists can assist children as they regain their footing: "The traumatic event is over; together, we occupy a benign here-and-now." Like sandbags by water's edge, these activities are our first defense in safeguarding the child from overwhelming affect. Since children need to connect with their therapists, several activities are also included toward this end.

My Own Personal Safety List

Sensory Census

Coat of Armor

Stop Right There

Osselet

Escape Velocity

My Own Personal Safety List

I worked with a woman who had been severely abused as a child, and her only memories of feeling safe and at ease were when she was alone, surrounded by a pine forest and the birds in the trees. You can learn a lot about the child's inner landscape through the creation of this list.

Objective: To promote self-soothing.

Materials and Preparation: Paper and pencil. Use the list provided below.

Activity: Ask the child what makes him feel safe and secure. You can provide a few examples to start off this list. If you like, use this activity as a jumping-off point to help children think through what it means to be supported in conversation—not being made fun of, reprimanded, or brushed off. When life gets stressful, there are "safe" people and "not-so-safe" people to talk to.

> ✓ **Tip:** The therapist's office may be the child's safest space, and the therapist may be the one who provides consistent caring over time. Show genuine affection for your clients and emphasize that your job is to keep the child and yourself safe.

I feel safe when I am:

1. Sitting in my mother's lap
2. Keeping the lights on
3. In my treehouse
4. Holding on to my favorite stuffed animal
5.
6.
7.
8.
9.
10.
11.
12.
13.
14.
15.

Sensory Census

While relaxation and imagery techniques focus the mind inward (potentially increasing awareness of the self), this activity strives to direct attention outward. Referred to as "grounding," trauma specialists endorse this approach for children struggling with the extreme emotional states of PTSD. While cognitive-behavioralists lay claim to this activity, it seems like basic meditation practice to me!

Objective: To cope with intense emotional states by "anchoring" to the here-and-now.

Materials and Preparation: This activity can be done anytime, anywhere, with no materials necessary.

Activity: A good part of the success of this activity depends on teaching the child when to utilize it. Together with the child, identify triggers or bodily feelings that would warrant doing the exercise. These could include hyperventilation, anxiety associated with flashbacks or intrusive memories, or tuning out and not feeling anything at all.

The activity itself is simple. Have the child really notice his surroundings, and itemize what is there in descriptive, silent sentences to himself. Suggest that he list as many things as possible; he should just keep going until he starts to feel better. Try to notice shapes, colors, sounds, what things might feel like. Mundane observations are fine and even a good idea.

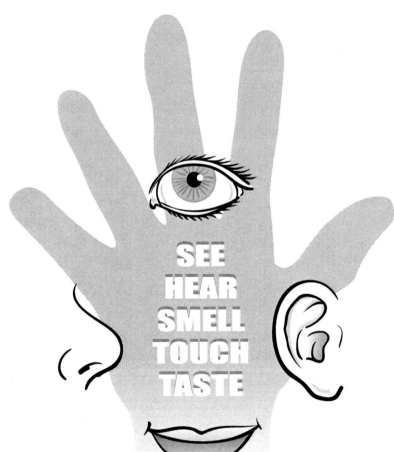

SEE
HEAR
SMELL
TOUCH
TASTE

For example, my list right now would go, "There's a black laptop straight ahead, lots of yellow and pink sticky notes all around, disks in disarray, an empty Dr. Brown's Black Cherry soda can, a post-card of a coyote turned on its side, a pocket accent pen, cold coffee in a plastic teal thermos, my "to-do" inbox piled to the top…" Well, it didn't work this time but it usually does.

> ✔ **Tip:** The child can also make a predetermined statement such as, "I am safe right now, what happened is in the past, I'm in the West Side playground on the third day of June."

Coat of Armor

 motional defenses. We all need mental tricks to take care of ourselves
'nk we are). Coat of Armor draws on the power of talismans—
...ic ability to strengthen and protect. In many cultures, people call to
...uer duress. Use the outline of the shield on the back of this page as a way to get
...ik about how they can protect themselves when they're feeling frightened or down.

Objective: To help children ward off painful words and actions.

Materials and Preparation: Use the outline of the shield provided.

Activity: Explain to the child the idea of a family crest or symbol. This is an abstract or realistic shape that represents the strength of the person and family. For example, it could be a fiery red lion standing on its hind legs (symbolizing fierce courage from an Irish coat of arms), or it could be a white with red T-shirt (as seen on the Guardian Angels of New York City). Have the child pick resonant symbols and colors, and draw them on the blank shield on page 6. Talk through why each symbol has meaning for the child.

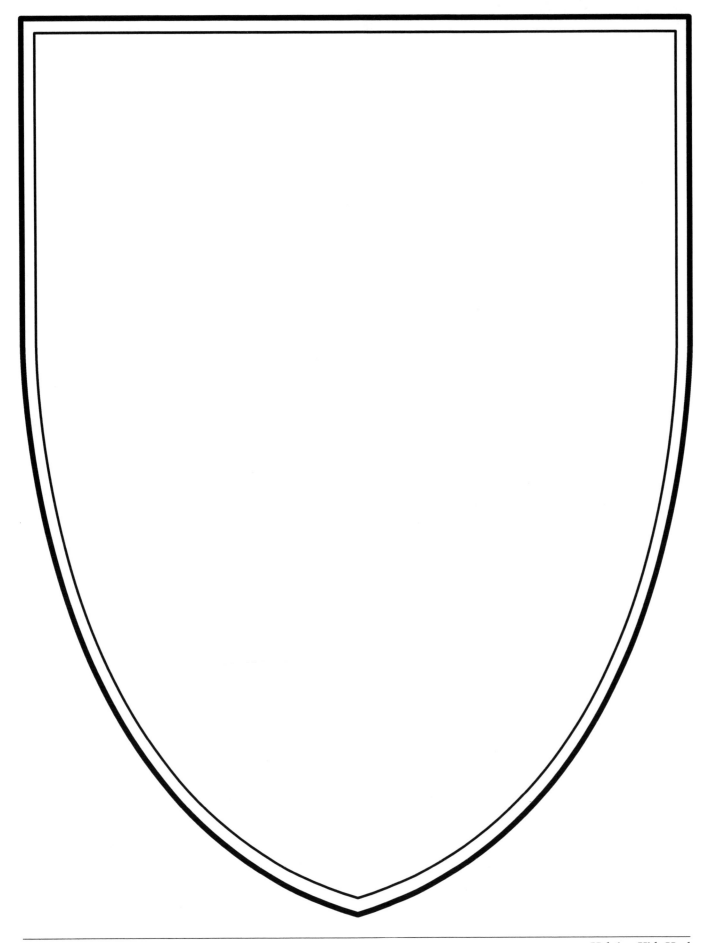

Stop Right There

This exercise is ridiculously simple, but it works. After disasters, people often have sounds and pictures that "intrude" into their minds over and over again. When these images come, it can be helpful to think of TV channels, and click to a less disturbing show. A conscious and deliberate effort to stop upsetting thoughts and replace them with others is key.

Objective: To learn a coping technique for handling flashbacks

Materials: The outline of a stop sign on the back of this page.

Activity: Suggest that the child color in the stop sign—use bright colors that will really get his attention! As you're sitting together, talk through when and how to use the stop sign. When bad memories come, tell the child to "stop," look at the sign, and think about something else.

Discuss with the child positive images that will make him feel better. One therapist I know helps children make lists of comforting things, category by category: people, places, things, foods, sounds, etc. Make sure to let kids know that most of the time these scary images go away by themselves. If for some reason they keep coming or get worse, it's important to tell an adult about it or (if possible) redouble efforts to imagine something more pleasant.

> ✓ **Tip:** To make the child's stop sign more realistic, you can use oak tag, contact paper, and a popsicle stick. Trace a 10" by 10" stop sign onto the oak tag, have the child color it, and then cut it out. Laminate the sign with the contact paper, making sure the edges of the contact paper are sticking to each other rather than the paper (to create stronger adhesion). As a final touch, put the popsicle stick in place.

Osselet

I recently visited Dwa Famn, an agency in Brooklyn committed to the human rights of Haitian women and girls. Staff there told me about this activity, akin to "jacks" in the United States. Osselet means ox bones and is played using just that! "If you grew up in Haiti, you played Osselet," said one social worker, praising this game for the way it creates normalcy.

Whenever possible, proactively seek out elements of a child's native culture to create a comfortable environment and establish rapport.

Objective: To aid in acculturation, relaxation, and connection.

Materials and Preparation: In Haiti, osselet are a by-product of the daily diet—the joint bones from oxen. Here, they are available at Haitian specialty stores. You need five osselet—or small bones or stones of any kind for this game.

Activity: Sit down together, with some space in between you, and throw all the bones down so they land somewhat close together. Take turns doing the following: pick up one bone, throw it up in the air, pick up one of the bones on the ground, and catch the first one before it hits the ground! In the next sequence, throw one bone in the air, keep one bone in your hand, pick up another bone from the ground, and catch the airborne bone—again, before it hits the ground. The first player keeps going in this fashion, holding two, three, and then four bones in her hand. If an osselet is dropped or missed, then the next person starts her turn.

> ✓ **Tip:** Losing a game can feel devastating to a fragile child. While you don't want to be obvious about letting kids win, think about ways to bolster particularly vulnerable children.

Escape Velocity

This activity is the brainchild of Joe Connor, who felt this book needed something tailor-made for kids who hate the idea of therapy! Joe lost his own father in a 1975 terrorist attack, and his cousin died in the World Trade Center disaster. He regrets he wasn't pushed to go to therapy back when he was a grieving nine-year-old (his tantrums and adamant refusal worked like a charm). It took decades for the family to really talk about what happened; Joe kept his feelings locked tightly inside.

Objective: To foster connection and comfort with the therapist.

Materials and Preparation: An armada of toy cars and rockets of all sizes, colors, and shapes.

Activity: Let the boy discover the toys and zoom them around however he likes. Both of you should steer, collide, race, screech to a halt, and take off again for quite some time. Follow the boy's lead, asking periodically what your vehicle should do next.

> ✔ **Tip:** Think about what crashes might represent in the life of the child. (Sometimes dramatic wrecks communicate feelings of helplessness, sometimes identification with the aggressor.) Don't bring in ambulances and good Samaritans right away, as it's good for children to get mayhem out of their system.

Consider asking the boy where he's headed. Joe imagines he might have used the race cars to "get the heck out of here," and the rockets to "fly up to see my father." He always played these kinds of games with his dad, and guesses a therapist's willingness to engage similarly would have increased his comfort level in treatment.

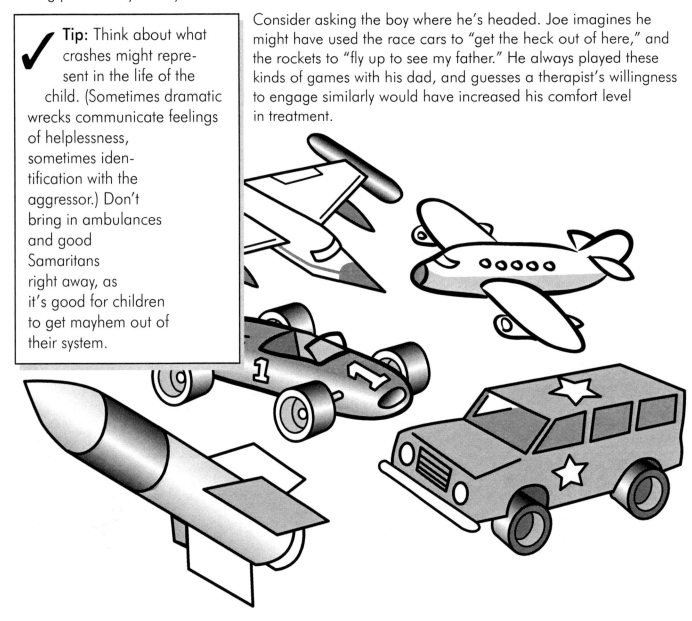

EASING INTO RELAXATION

These activities help children cope with tension and stress, and can be used to deescalate emotions if they spiral out of control. Before children do the "work" of therapy, they need to find ways to modulate the intense physiological reactions that may arise. Reestablishing safety and the ability to let down one's guard are prerequisites for treatment, and paradoxically, the end result. Let these activities assume the familiar quality of ritual, and return to them again and again during the child's healing process.

The Rag Doll

Tense and Release Classic

Big Bubbles, No Troubles

Dreamscape in Green

Do-it-Yourself Listening Booth

Take Me Away!

The Rag Doll

This activity is a classic, and variations abound. The idea is to help children find out where tension "lives" in their bodies and shake out this tension like a rag doll.

Most of us ignore our pain, letting it hover half in and out of consciousness. Through example, we can model for children compassion for our own distress.

Objective: To relax and have fun! To learn where stress resides in this child's body.

Materials and Preparation: Just yourselves and your knotted-up, tight-as-a-board muscles. It helps to have a Raggedy Ann or Andy around to demonstrate.

Activity: Say to the child that sometimes it feels good to pretend to be a rag doll, loose and floppy without any tension anywhere. Start by shaking out your legs together, then your arms, then your neck and shoulder area and your torso. Silliness is encouraged; go ahead and do this one right alongside the child.

It's a challenge to be totally limp and relaxed in your legs and stay standing up! See how well you both master it; you can also try being sitting, lying-down, and dancing-around rag dolls. (A rag doll taking a nap is the ultimate in relaxed.) Ask if the child feels stiff or tight anywhere in particular, and then give that place extra positive attention and care.

✔ **Tip:** Play music and have the child practice a rag doll dance at different speeds.

Tense and Release Classic

This exercise is an old standard, used in stress reduction groups from Santa Monica to Santiago. It can be used on its own or as a lead-in to other activities. As children bring awareness to their breath and each muscle group, they are learning to gently focus their attention—paving the way for learning of all kinds.

Objective: To help children relax.

Materials and Preparation: A mat or soft rug to lie on. Enough space so the child can lie down comfortably. Some therapists like to play calming music in the background.

Activity: Get into position, with the child sitting or lying down and you seated nearby. Explain that you're going to do an exercise that will last about ten minutes and that it's fine to stop at any time.

> ✔ **Tip:** Consider the child's background; if there is a history of abuse by adults, this activity may make children feel vulnerable. Let children choose whether they would like to sit or lie down. Wherever they are most comfortable is where the activity will work best!

Demonstrate tensing and releasing—when parts of the body are tensed the muscles get as tight as you can make them. Then, when muscles are released, they get loose and limp like spaghetti.

Have children start by noticing where tension is in their bodies, noticing their breath going in and out, and letting go of thoughts and worries. Beginning at the toes, work your way through all of the child's major muscle groups, with toes and feet first, then calves, then thighs, etc. You can use language like, "Notice your toes and how they're feeling, take a deep breath and tense up your toes as hard as you can… hold it for a moment… and now, let go of the tension in your toes as you breathe out."

Make sure not to forget neck and jaws and forehead! Once you have reached the very top of the child's head, work your way back down again ending with a wiggle of the child's toes. After the exercise, talk over how the child felt before the activity, and how the child feels now.

Talk over different times and places the child could use this activity on their own—for instance, it is effective in helping children fall asleep.

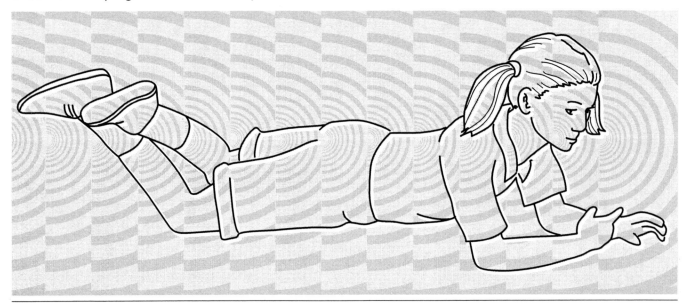

Big Bubbles, No Troubles

This is really a deep breathing exercise, but you don't have to call it that. As children learn to blow large bubbles, they are also learning diaphragmatic breathing. Therapists use all sorts of bubble blowing techniques to demonstrate the mechanics of optimum oxygenation!

Objective: To distinguish between shallow, rapid breathing and the deep breathing that promotes relaxation.

Materials and Preparation: Bubble stuff capable of blowing HUGE bubbles. Or, bubble stuff for "permanent" bubbles—ones that are hard to pop. A large room or outdoor space where splattered bubble stuff is not a problem.

Activity: First, ask the child to make the smallest bubbles he can. After practicing this for a while, suggest to the child that he make the largest bubbles he can—this will require taking a very deep breath all the way into the stomach, and blowing out very slowly and carefully! It's fine to throw in some psycho-education: "Some people feel more cool, calm, and collected when they breathe deeply, and when they pay attention to their breath." Extol the benefits of breathing through one's nose (this activates the lower portion of the diaphragm).

> ✓ **Tip:** You might have the child place his hands on his chest and diaphragm to see how they alternately rise and fall during deep breathing.

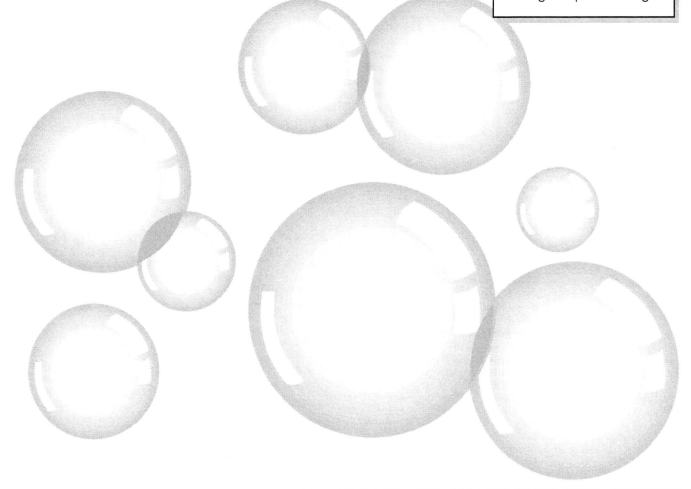

Dreamscape in Green

This activity comes from Jude Ornstein, who used it with children in an inpatient psychiatric hospital setting. Jude is a firm believer that art therapists must do each and every arts activity themselves before trying it with children. They can then gauge how long the activity is likely to take, how the materials work, and most importantly, when emotionally difficult moments might arise.

"As children get involved in their work, they can feel extremely exposed," Jude says. "Make sure they have their right to privacy. I always welcome their communication, but they don't have to talk about anything they put down."

Objective: To engage in a soothing, tactile activity. To create an image for self-soothing.

Materials and Preparation: Dry pastels or colored chalks and paper. A variety of landscape pictures or paintings, taken from calendars, stationery, photographs, or any other source. These images should be beautiful, eclectic, and calming.

Activity: Let the child select one of the landscape images, and explain the project: She is going to draw and smudge a scene evocative of the chosen image. The idea is to create the feeling of the place, not an exact duplication. Have the child begin, showing her how to smudge pastels if necessary.

Don't let children blow pastel dust into the air, as it's not good for them to breathe.

> ✔ **Tip:** If a child tears up her artwork in frustration, save the pieces and—together with the child—use them to create something beautiful at a later date.

Do-It-Yourself Listening Booth

Most children are familiar with the listening stations in music stores that enable customers to hear music before they buy it—track one, track two, track three, and of course those padded headphones. In this activity, one corner of your office will be transformed into an Oz-like listening booth.

Objective: To help children discover soothing music.

Materials and Preparation: Set up a corner of your office or recreation room, perhaps using a curtain or partition. Have a CD player and about four or five CDs that you've preselected. These could be new age music, sounds of nature, vocal music—whatever you think might work.

Activity: Explain the scenario, then play a bit of each kind of music. Have your young "customer" evaluate which piece helps him feel calm. Remember, the customer is always right and sometimes none of the options do the trick. If all your choices fall flat, invite the child to bring in a musical selection of his own as an alternative. Ideally, record the child's selection and present it to him as a gift.

If cost is an issue, you can just flip through channels on the radio.

> ✓ **Tip:** A therapist I know swears by Metallica and Def Leopard as calming influences. For some kids, raucous music is settling because it expresses what they feel on the inside. Staying hyped-up and agitated can be a way for kids to defend against the pain underneath.

Take Me Away!

Children can use relaxation imagery in just the same way adults do. The point is to help children develop their imaginations, so they can—with disciplined practice—access an oasis of well-being no matter what the outside world brings. I heard about a boy who felt best alone on the beach, watching layers of sand get pulled out to sea; this memory became the basis for his "safe place."

Objective: To help children cope with emotional or physical pain by reinforcing an internal sanctuary. To lay the groundwork for hope for a better future.

Materials and Preparation: A mat to lie down on if you choose to do guided imagery. As always, model the calm and stillness you wish to impart to the child.

Activity: The central part of this activity entails helping the child identify a special place from her own life and fully elaborating the feeling of this spot. This place should be a sanctuary—serene, intimate, and beautiful. It can be contemporary or mistily recalled from a time long ago. What does this place look like, smell like, sound like, etc.? What exactly makes this place feel safe to the child? Then, you can ask the child to write about her chosen spot, draw it, or listen to a guided script (created by you) detailing a slow, rich approach and entry to the special place. In all instances, encourage the child to keep with her the peacefulness of the sanctuary even once the exercise is done.

✔ **Tip:** If you're doing guided imagery for the first time with a child, make sure to practice a lot beforehand!

If you choose to do guided imagery with a child, provide the basic route of the journey while encouraging small individual choices at certain junctures. So, for example, you might say, "You enter the room we talked about, with the walls painted silver and gold, and your favorite CD playing…" Children need opportunities to "fill in blanks" in their mind's eye, personalizing their journey and letting sensory images seep under their skin.

LEARNING ABOUT FEELINGS

These activities help children identify and understand various emotions. Reading and interpreting emotions is like a language unto itself; we therapists can serve as translators as children sort out feelings in themselves and others. In addition, we can introduce the notion that children's emotions and reactions make perfect sense, given what they have experienced. The ability to understand feelings is vital when maneuvering through painful emotional terrain.

Word Search

Batten Down the Hatches!

What They Were Thinking

Worried Sick

Tragic/Comic

Word Search

It's hard to get a handle on our feelings but it's a basic therapeutic principle that the ability to name feelings helps us gain control over them. The more we understand about the subtleties of our emotions, the better we can tolerate them and realize their fluid, ephemeral nature.

Objective: To help children develop knowledge about emotions.

Materials and Preparation: See the word search on the back of this page.

Activity: Search for the following words in the puzzle on page 22: sad, mad, glad, gleeful, ecstatic, doldrums, furious, silly, guilty, carefree, anxious, excited, confused, numb, irritated, hopeful, nostalgic, content, wistful.

Explain any words the child might not have heard of, and talk through times you both have felt these ways. Gradually, you will develop a common language about feelings, so you can match various states of being with their precise descriptions and typical triggers.

> ✔ **Tip:** Don't worry if these words seem large or complex. Recognizing them is the first step, and you can chime in as much as you need to.

Y	T	L	I	U	G	E	G	K	Y	G	P
T	W	N	S	P	H	B	M	N	D	L	T
M	I	S	E	Z	W	C	M	E	O	E	I
Q	S	H	N	T	K	R	T	M	L	E	R
D	T	W	A	M	N	I	B	F	D	F	R
M	F	Z	A	N	C	O	N	U	R	U	I
C	U	D	T	X	X	M	C	R	U	L	T
A	L	Y	E	F	W	I	G	I	M	L	A
R	S	L	V	S	T	N	O	O	S	M	T
E	T	L	J	A	U	K	M	U	Q	D	E
F	H	I	T	B	C	F	V	S	S	A	D
R	L	S	T	B	M	U	N	M	R	L	K
E	C	M	L	U	F	E	P	O	H	G	R
E	N	O	S	T	A	L	G	I	C	K	F

Find these feelings words:

ANXIOUS • CAREFREE • CONFUSED • CONTENT • DOLDRUMS • ECSTATIC • EXCITED
FURIOUS • GLAD • GLEEFUL • GUILTY • HOPEFUL • IRRITATED • MAD • NOSTALGIC
NUMB • SAD • SILLY • WISTFUL

Batten Down the Hatches!

The barometer was invented in Italy in the early 16th century as a way to measure air pressure and thus predict weather. It was often used on seafaring vessels; picture a 20-foot wooden boat, buffeted by huge waves and sheets of driving rain in the middle of the vast Atlantic.

The weather/emotions analogy is apt on so many levels. We're caught off guard by our emotions, and stymied when it's rainy and sunny at the same time. With the help of modern instrumentation (pictured on the back of this page), get a heads-up regarding children's emotions.

Objective: To help children realize that one can feel each emotion "a little" or "a lot."

Materials and Preparation: The barometer on the back of this page.

Activity: Look at the barometer together with the child. Explain that it's a way to measure the amount of feelings a person has—for the case of argument, anger. Ten represents the most angry you could ever feel, and zero represents not feeling any anger at all. Where on the scale is the child's anger level? You can ask children to refer to the barometer when that particular emotion comes up during the session, or you can have children do a quick "check-in" as they arrive.

> ✓ **Tip:** Make sure you don't sound disapproving or shocked if the child expresses high levels of sadness, anger, etc. You also might want to mention that sometimes people feel unemotional altogether, only to feel high levels of several emotions the very next day! This is a great time to model curiosity and acceptance of whatever happens.

Try this: Draw your own arrow to whichever number shows how strong your feelings are right now.

What They Were Thinking

I like this activity for its projective possibilities; children provide glimpses of what they are feeling or reveal ways that they inadvertently distort incoming information. Studies indicate that children who have been abused are more likely to see anger and aggression in the faces of others.

Rachelle Kammer, a specialist in public education about mental health issues, told me about this activity.

Objective: To help children recognize feelings and cultivate empathy.

Materials and Preparation: About twenty or thirty photographs of people that you have cut out of magazines. Make sure faces are clearly visible and that there is expressive body language. Find as great a range of expressions as possible in people of all ages and walks of life; images that are captivating, intriguing, or mysterious are that much better. Put the images into a box or bag.

Activity: Have the child draw an image out of the box and look at it carefully. Ask the child to tell you a story about what that person is thinking or feeling. Write down the story. Let the whole story emerge before you provide your perspective. This helps the child feel understood and heard and allows you to gather as much information as possible. After the child has fully expressed himself, it's fine to share what it is that you observe about the photographs.

> ✓ **Tip:** Make sure your perspective is given in the spirit of dialogue, not correction, or the child may be reluctant to open up in the future.

Worried Sick

L ots of children somaticize their emotional pain—feeling anger as a headache, worry as a stomachache, sadness as tiredness, and so on. This can also reflect cultural differences.

Objective: To help children make connections between physical discomfort and emotional pain.

Materials and Preparation: A large piece of butcher block paper—large enough for the child to lie down on and have his body traced. Colored markers or paints.

Activity: Have the child match up three or four feelings with corresponding colors of paint. For instance, red might mean "angry," blue might mean "calm," and so on. Using the outline of the child's body traced onto paper, instruct the child to paint each color on the traced body where it belongs. Be attentive to the child's decisions about each color's placement. Reflect back on what the child does, using language like, "I notice you've put a big red patch up all around where your head is. It seems like when you feel angry, your head feels like it's going to explode. Do I have that right…?"

> ✓ **Tip:** This activity is often used by sexual abuse evaluators. Consider the implications of colors placed around the genital area, especially if supported by corroborating material.

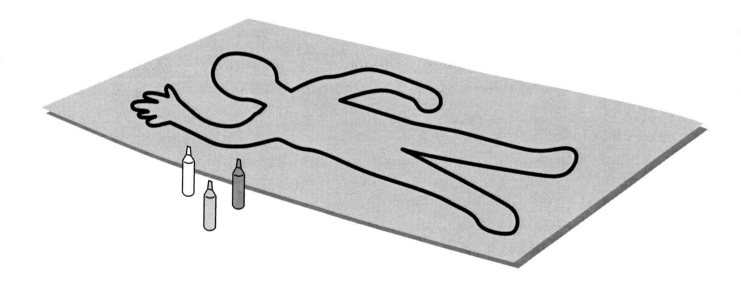

Tragic/Comic

This poignant activity can open up discussion about the idea of defenses and hiding feelings. It is useful for all children, especially those who have difficulty acknowledging negative emotions like anger or sadness. I learned about this activity from the staff at the Coalition for Asian American Children and Families.

Objective: To illustrate that sometimes the way people present themselves isn't how they feel on the inside.

Materials: White, plastic masks available from crafts stores. Acrylic paints in a variety of colors, and brushes.

Activity: Propose to the child that she decorate two faces, one on each side of the mask. Have the outside of the mask represent the way the child thinks she is generally perceived, and the inside of the mask represent the way that she really feels. (You might need to do this in two separate sessions, so the paint can dry in between.) Discussion can include gentle queries about what makes the child feel the way she does on the inside, and what would happen if people really knew how she felt.

✓ **Tip:** It's a privilege to be trusted with deeply felt feelings. Convey to the child (through actions and affect as well as words) how much of a gift it is for you to learn about her vulnerable feelings.

STUCK AND UNSTUCK

Throughout the world, people sing, dance and move as a way of transcending trauma. These are physical exercises to help emotions flow through children's bodies and be released. As we all know, children would rather cavort than talk about feelings. These activities build on the vocabulary of emotions and are reassuring to kids: Maybe therapy won't be so bad after all.

Web of Connection

Makin' Rain

Crocodile Tears

Water Percussion

Popping Like Popcorn

Nature Charades

Web of Connection

This activity is from Amber Gray, a Colorado-based therapist who has worked with child refugees and torture victims from around the world. She says the children she sees are often socially withdrawn and have a hard time handling stimulation without flooding or "freezing." "They feel stuck," she says. "Trauma is a fixation of energy." Amber finds this activity (based on remembering the path of the beanbag) promotes connection and frees the flow of energy around a room.

This activity is for use with a group.

Objective: To cooperate, and increase tolerance for charged activities.

Materials and Preparation: A soft ball or beanbag.

Activity: Sit together in a circle. Toss the beanbag to a child, saying his or her name. This child will toss it to another (saying his or her name), who will toss it to another and so on, with no child receiving the beanbag twice. When every child has caught the beanbag, it is thrown back to you. Do the exercise once again, to test whether each child remembers the pattern (the beanbag moving from child to child in the same order).

Now the fun begins! Try the game again—staying within the pattern—but this time have the beanbag be slow (or fast, hot, cold, sad, happy, etc.) Another variation is to add beanbags, so that a second, third, and (up to the number of children participating) beanbags are in play at the same time.

Amber remembers doing Web of Connection with a group of child refugees in Denver. One eight-year-old boy clenched up and kept dropping the beanbag. A younger girl came and sat next to him, told him to breathe and to keep his eyes on the beanbag. "It's a happy beanbag!" she said, and soon he could catch it.

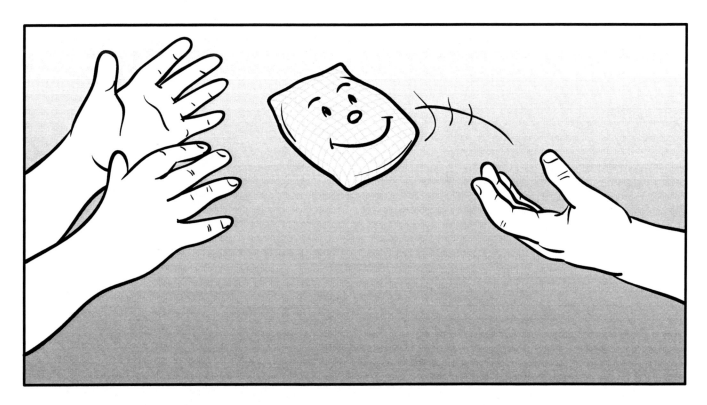

Makin' Rain

This is a favorite at camps and after-school programs. The release of movement and making noise helps children feel calmer and more centered. It works best with about eight children, but can be adapted for just one.

This activity is for use with a group.

Objective: To achieve catharsis, physical and emotional.

Materials and Preparation: A place where children can be as loud as possible with no recrimination.

Activity: Gather children into a circle (and be part of the circle yourself). Together, you are going to create the sound of a summer rainstorm, gently approaching, getting stronger and stronger, whipping up into a frenzy, letting loose sheets and buckets of rain, then slowly softening and softening and going away completely. You will be the leader for each step in the rainstorm. Each time you introduce a new type of sound, this noise will be "passed around" the circle from one child to the next. There is no talking during this activity.

Begin by slowly rubbing your hands together. The child to the right of you then rubs his hands together, then the child to the right of that child, and so on and so forth until all the children are rubbing their hands. Each child should wait for a few seconds before doing the new movement. When the child on your left is doing the movement you have started with (it has traveled all the way around the circle), then you can start with the next one.

After rubbing your hands together, gently snap your fingers. Then snap louder. Then clap your hands together, then slap your thighs, then stomp your feet. Let the snapping and clapping and stomping reach a crescendo, then reverse the order and one by one do quieter and quieter movements, ending at last with the gentle rub of the fingers and then trailing into silence.

Crocodile Tears

Adults often forget that those tediously familiar emotions—"Here I go, feeling stressed out again"—were once strange and inexplicable sensations. This activity is a fun way to get a group of kids thinking about the physical sensations connected to various feelings. I learned about it from our Comfort for Kids trainer Karen Bernstein, who had a previous incarnation on the stage. She remembered this exercise from acting class.

This activity is for use with a group.

Objective: To broaden children's vocabularies and physiological understanding of feelings. To lay the groundwork for empathy.

Materials and Preparation: Be ready to call out a list of about twenty or thirty different "emotion" words. A large kid-friendly space is also key.

Activity: Explain the game: you are going to call out a list of different emotions, naming a new one every thirty seconds or so. When children hear each one, they must act it out as dramatically as possible. After the exercise, sit in a circle with the children and "debrief" what you've done, emotion by emotion. For example, when you called out "sad," did they feel heavy or light? How did their faces look, and were their backs and shoulders hunched? What about their voices? Did it help to remember an actual time that they felt this way? Can they remember such a time now?

> ✓ **Tip:** A variation is to have one group of children watch another, then switch roles. Afterward, have children share with you what they observed and felt.

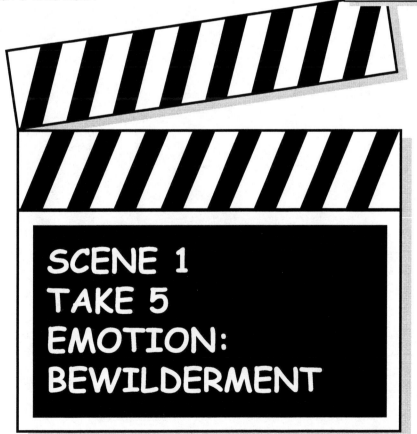

SCENE 1
TAKE 5
EMOTION:
BEWILDERMENT

Water Percussion

I recently heard about a singular piece of music, The Concerto for Water Percussion and Orchestra. Based entirely on the element of water, this concerto debuted in Singapore using invented "instruments" such as basins of water struck by hand and by gong, water shakers, water bells, and water phones. According to reviewers, the piece ended with a "gigantic, gushing waterfall effect."

This activity integrates physical movement, the use of all five senses, and the healing properties of water!

Objective: To achieve physical release and emotional expression through sound.

Materials and Preparation: Containers of various shapes and sizes for water. Multiple sinks, faucets, and hoses, if possible. Spoons and other utensils to use as gongs. A metronome. You'll want to try this in a room immune to water damage, or better yet, outside.

Activity: Together with the child, create the instruments by filling the containers with water. First, explore the wide range of sounds that are possible to make with the items at your disposal. After you've played around for a while, suggest to the child that you compose a piece to express a particular mood or a progression of moods— say, grumpy to sassy to filled with anticipation. Ask the child what "instrument" you should play, and how you should play it (or them). Seek to create a piece with different tones and textures, about three to four minutes long. You can use the metronome to keep on rhythm, setting whatever speed is appropriate.

Popping Like Popcorn

This activity is from Joyce Weiss, a specialist in the expressive arts. She uses physical activity in combination with mental imagery to create a sense of catharsis. Especially with children who have had their bodies controlled and violated, physical mastery is important—feeling alive in one's own skin instead of cut off and deadened.

This activity is for use with a group.

Objective: To let pain be released from the body. To practice imagery that stresses cleansing, upward movement, lightness, and expansion.

Materials and Preparation: A large space in which children can move around energetically and freely.

Activity: Explain the exercise to children: they are going to act out the words and phrases you say. Encourage them to be as lively and vivid and energetic as possible, and to really imagine being these things. If you like, choose one of the children to do sound effects. During opportune moments, ask them about the images and feelings that come up. How does each activity apply to a particular child's life?

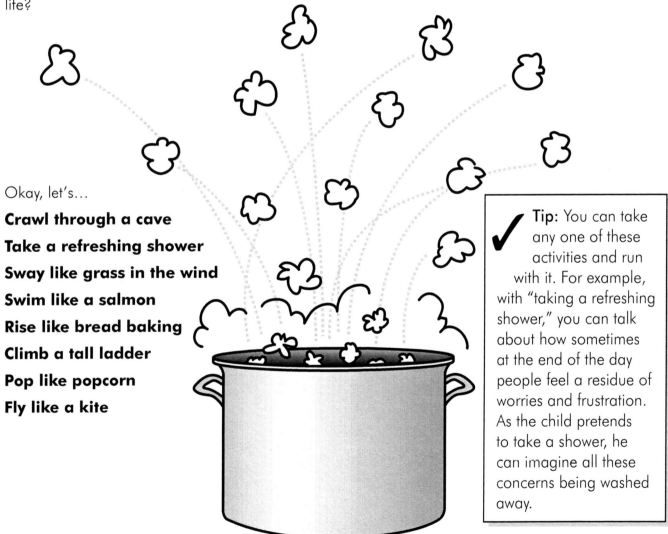

Okay, let's…

Crawl through a cave

Take a refreshing shower

Sway like grass in the wind

Swim like a salmon

Rise like bread baking

Climb a tall ladder

Pop like popcorn

Fly like a kite

✔ **Tip:** You can take any one of these activities and run with it. For example, with "taking a refreshing shower," you can talk about how sometimes at the end of the day people feel a residue of worries and frustration. As the child pretends to take a shower, he can imagine all these concerns being washed away.

Nature Charades

This is an activity I learned about from an international relief agency working in India. It can be adapted for children of all ages, and is useful after natural disasters. You'd be amazed at how well children duplicate the energy of a monsoon!

This activity is for use with a group.

Objective: To learn facts about the natural world, express feelings, and gain physical release.

Materials and Preparation: Pieces of paper, pens, and a hat or other container. Bone up on your earth science, figuring out simple, clear ways to explain complex phenomena. Write the words for different forces of nature (see below for suggestions) on slips of paper, and put them in the hat.

✓ **Tip:** It's great to use this game in a preventive way— i.e., before anything bad has happened. The more knowledge children have about the world around them, the better! Nature sets a great example of regeneration.

Activity: One by one, have children reach in and grab a piece of paper. Once they've read the word written there, they should act out their understanding of it. The remaining children can try to guess what the word is. Elicit discussion after each child has performed; what do children know about the phenomenon in question? Have they ever seen/experienced it? What are their ideas about why it happens?

Words to consider including are "wind," "tide," "hurricane," "mist," "thunderstorm," "rockslide," "undertow," "sunshine," "tornado," "drought," etc. Make sure to include positive natural forces, as well as scary and destructive ones.

WHAT ACTUALLY HAPPENED

These activities help ensure that the child has a baseline understanding of the traumatic event. They check the child's knowledge of the facts, and address distortions and confusion potentially impeding recovery and peace of mind. During these activities and those in the next section, be sure to monitor the intensity of children's reactions and make a transition if need be. Plan your "exit strategy" ahead of time with activities stressing safety, relaxation, or empowerment.

Who, What, Where, When...Why?

A Thousand Words

Before and After

Dear Abby

Who, What, Where, When...Why?

As a New York City resident during The World Trade Center disaster, the number of times I've gone over where I was (West 4th St. and 6th Ave., heading for the A Express) and heard other people's stories is probably in the thousands. After disasters, people feel a need to talk about exactly where they were and what they were doing—and it's helpful to do so. Traumatic memories can have that "frozen in time" quality or keep coming back again and again. Reviewing the facts in a gentle, safe setting can begin to shake them loose.

Objective: To help children process trauma. To ensure that children aren't distorting or misunderstanding information.

Materials and Preparation: A pencil or pen and paper. Feel free to alter the questions if appropriate.

Activity: With the child, answer the questions below.

Where were you when the event happened?

What were you doing just before it happened?

When did you find out?

Who let you know what happened?

Why do you think it happened?

> ✔ **Tip:** One task of the therapist is to help children bridge the moment just before a traumatic event with the moment just after. Often there is a sense of dramatic rupture, a "before" and "after" and never the twain shall meet. Through conversation and play about the entire sequence, the child regains a sense of the continuity of time.

Who What Where What When Why

A Thousand Words

Because children are developmentally immature—and simply have had less time to observe the workings of the world—they often make assumptions. Children might conclude that they themselves had a role in bringing about the misfortune because they misbehaved that day. Or, they might think the event is happening over and over again when they watch repeat footage on TV.

Objective: To establish a basic understanding of what has happened. To ensure children's thinking is free from misplaced guilt or confusion.

Materials and Preparation: Paper and pencils or pens.

Activity: Ask the child to draw an image of the frightening thing that happened. After the finishing touches have been made, ask him or her to describe the picture in words. Write down on the back of the sheet of paper exactly what the child tells you. Gentle questions can bring to the surface any distortions in cause and effect.

✔ **Tip:** Lots of people are tempted to protect children from the truth. While it is good to use age-appropriate language and avoid grisly details, it's not good to out-and-out lie as children almost unfailingly find out.

Variations: Consider using drawing exercises with younger children, and a mix of drawing and writing exercises with older children. Here, we're after full, rich description so if the child just writes a sentence or two, nudge toward greater elaboration. Whatever is generated is the starting point for your discussion!

Before and After

This activity is best to use with children who are one step removed from a tragic event—say, a community-wide disaster in which no one in the child's immediate family was hurt. When the "after" is obvious and devastating—after the murder of a child's mother, for example—merely posing the question will rupture the therapeutic alliance. As in, "Lady, you have no clue about my life."

Objective: To help children process the event. To help them realize the things they still have.

Materials: Paper and pencil.

Activity: Fold a piece of paper in half, and label one column "before" and one "after." Ask the child to make a list of the way things were before the incident. Then, fill out the other side of the paper, the "after" list. Look for ripple effects, small and large changes, community-wide impacts. Also, encourage the child to consider what things have stayed the same. While the column on the right may end up being a long and sad list, help bring to the fore positive outcomes such as people helping each other, etc.

Dear Abby

It's hard for all of us to get our minds around cataclysmic events. For children, they can be mind-boggling. This activity can provide a forum for considering daunting topics such as the existence of evil, the mysteries of chance, and the paradoxical nature of religious faith.

This activity is for use with a group.

Objectives: To find out what children's questions are and help them find answers.

Materials and Preparation: A large hat (or just a paper bag), a bunch of torn-up strips of paper, and something to write with. Explain the concept of "Dear Abby"—for decades, readers wrote in to her daily newspaper column, posing questions without signing their real names. Often readers described situations that they were too embarrassed to reveal to their family or friends.

Activity: Ask the child to write down as many questions about the event as he or she can, and put the strips into the hat. (If necessary, be the transcriber.) You should write down questions too—ones you think might be on the child's mind, ones you've heard other children asking, or whatever your gut tells you is the most perplexing aspect of what happened. (Inform children that you're including questions you've heard from other kids.) Shake the hat up with gusto, and start pulling out questions one by one. Answer the questions together; try to get a feel for what the child thinks the answer is—then fill in, assist with misperceptions, or elaborate wherever need be. Remember, some questions have no good or satisfying answers, and it's okay to say we don't know!

✔ **Tip:** The nice thing about this activity is that it creates the illusion of anonymity, so children can ask questions they consider dumb, morbid, or just plain weird. Even when children clamor to "own" their questions, it's best to stick to the ground rules.

Super Mom in Dallas · In a rut · Hip Granny in Memphis · Angry In-law · Out of answers · Mad as heck · Eating My Words · Grateful in Gainesville · Dear Abby · Wallflower in Missouri

NG FEELINGS

vent and the accompanying feelings; without taking this
"You have to go through the bad parts to get to the other
g of this section. Expressing scary, overwhelming, and dark
is central to the process of healing. It's no easy task to
witnessing is so important. This time the child is not alone.

aphic Timeline

.. Huh?

'izza Pie

n the Blank

The Shape of Grief

Baggage Check

T. P. Artillery

Bouncing for Columbine

Seismographic Timeline

Youth Communication in New York City has lots of initiatives, including a monthly magazine by and for kids in foster care. Mostly focused on teens, the agency's philosophy—that youth benefit by hearing "I've been where you are now" stories from peers—is also applicable to younger children.

Youth Communication staff use this activity—a timeline that captures the ups and downs of each person's life story—in a group setting so staff and teens can get to know each other. It's especially poignant when used with children in foster care, who have known so much upheaval and transience.

Objective: To obtain baseline knowledge about important events in a child's life.

Materials and Preparation: A sheet of butcher block paper five or six feet long and markers. Tape the paper securely to the wall at about the child's eye level. (You can also use a piece of 11" by 17" paper and do the activity sitting at a desk.)

Activity: Together with the child, draw a thick horizontal line beginning at zero (when the child was born) and ending with the child's current age. Make marks representing each year of the child's life, labeling as you go. Next, gently ask about significant events (moves, deaths, milestones, accomplishments) that have occurred.

Once the date has been located on the line, have the child assess how positive or upsetting each event was, on a scale of one to ten. Positive events are measured upwards (above the timeline), and negative events are measured downwards (below the line). Make a prominent dot indicating intensity. At the end of the exercise, go ahead and connect all the dots.

> ✓ **Tip:** It's important not to make assumptions. For example, the death of a child's grandmother could be devastating or barely a blip on the screen.

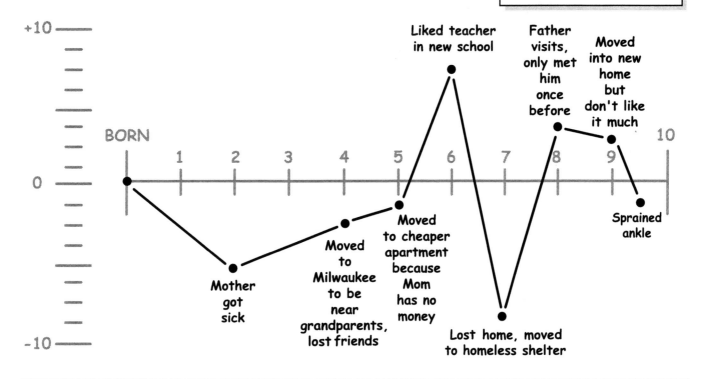

...Huh?

Barbara Golby works with HIV-positive children, helping them to understand and cope with their illness. One girl was thirteen when she learned of her diagnosis; her mother had died when she was seven. Barbara tried everything to reach this girl but to no avail. Finally, Barbara hit upon the idea of asking her to draw her face when she found out she had HIV. The girl drew a face with eyes wide with surprise, the mouth gaping open. In a thought bubble overhead floated the single word, "huh?"

Objective: To identify and process feelings experienced during charged times.

Materials and Preparation: Colored pens and paper.

Activity: This one really depends on timing. During conversations about upsetting events, a moment may arise when you have the urge to ask, "How did you feel?" but you know the reaction will be a mute silence or shrug. This is the perfect time to introduce this exercise. As Barbara did, simply ask the child to draw her face when first taking in the news.

> ✔ **Tip:** As the child is drawing his face, he is feeling and processing the emotions associated with the event. Allow plenty of time and create a quiet, calm atmosphere during this exercise.

Pizza Pie

This activity is another great way to engage children who get annoyed by all those touchy-feely feeling words and adults earnestly asking, "How are you feeling?" When there has been an incident that elicits complex or contradictory emotions, this technique is particularly useful.

Objective: To identify feelings associated with an event and to realize one can have lots of feelings at the same time.

Materials and Preparation: A round circle traced onto a larger piece of paper (the pizza pie), pens for coloring, and small squares of paper. Select whatever event the child is currently working on (for example, "when my sister was beat up and ended up in the ICU") and write down simple words for the feelings you believe were elicited on the small squares of paper, one feeling per piece. Review these feelings with the child to make sure he knows what they are.

Activity: Present the circle and the pile of feelings to the child, and refer to the event in question. ("Remember how you told me about your sister being hurt walking home after school…") Explain that he is going to divide up this pizza into slices, one slice for every feeling he has about the event. The big variable here is size; he can make very tiny slivers of pizza for feelings that are minute, and huge pieces that wouldn't even fit in your mouth for feelings that are gigantic. After all the slices are drawn, label each piece with the emotion and color it in.

> ✔ **Tip:** Make sure to normalize having a whole range of feelings—mad and a little glad at the same time, for example.

The pile of papers with feelings written on them are just to get the child started. Make sure to emphasize that there may be important feelings that you left out or feelings you put in that he doesn't have at all.

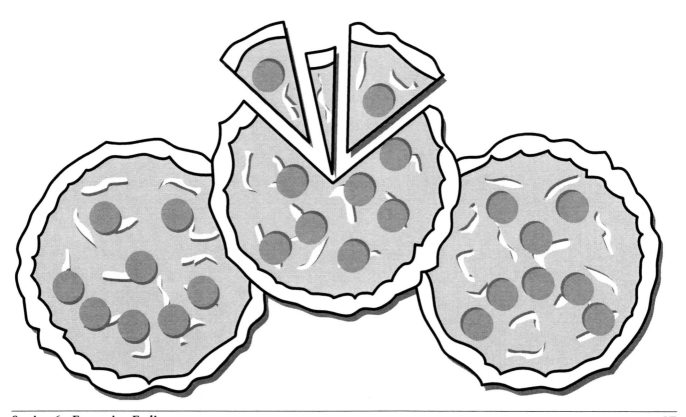

Fill in the Blank

This activity works to address something specific that negatively impacts a child's life. The idea is to provide a symbol of this negative influence, to which the child can respond impressionistically. For example, when a child has a family member who is an alcoholic, the symbol might be the outline of a bottle. When a child has been hurt in an accident, the symbol might be the outline of a cast.

Objective: To express feelings and associations about a situation in the child's life.

Materials: A large, blank piece of paper with an outlined symbol on it. Colored pens, markers, or pencils. Use your knowledge of the child's life to make the symbol that is the basis for this activity, or create the symbol together with the child.

Activity: Begin by saying something like, "You know, the other day you mentioned how you don't like it when you come home and you find your mother intoxicated and passed out on the kitchen floor. Kids can have a lot of different feelings when their parents drink..." Suggest to the child that she fill in the symbol with all the colors, words, or images that come to mind when she thinks about drinking (or whatever it is the symbol represents). Make sure to stay engaged and observant as the child works, and ask clarifying questions as needed.

> ✔ **Tip:** It's best if you decide together what the symbol should be, so it arises organically from your work together. Otherwise, the child may feel ashamed and exposed.

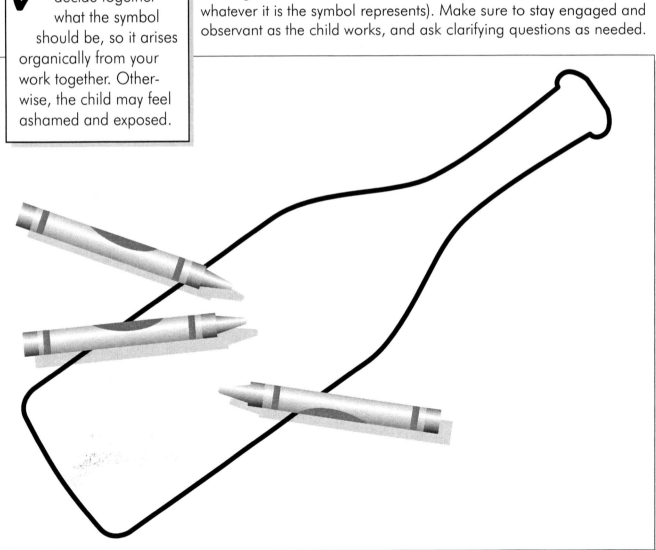

The Shape of Grief

At the Rock Creek Cemetery in Washington, D.C. is a sculpture called "Grief" which dates from the late 1800s. Henry Adams had it commissioned after the death of his wife because he needed an outlet for his immense sorrow.

This activity helps children express their own grief. Because the medium is clay, the activity also allows children physical release through hitting, rolling, and pounding.

Objective: To express and communicate emotional pain.

Materials and Preparation: Clay and an appropriate workplace.

Activity: First, allow the child to play with the clay in a nondirective way. At an opportune moment, suggest to the child that he make a sculpture that shows the sadness inside him. As always, consider making statements about what you see. "It must be hard to carry around such a heavy, torn-up lump of sadness." Some clinicians like to do this exercise once at the beginning of treatment, and then again toward the end. Notice whatever changes take place.

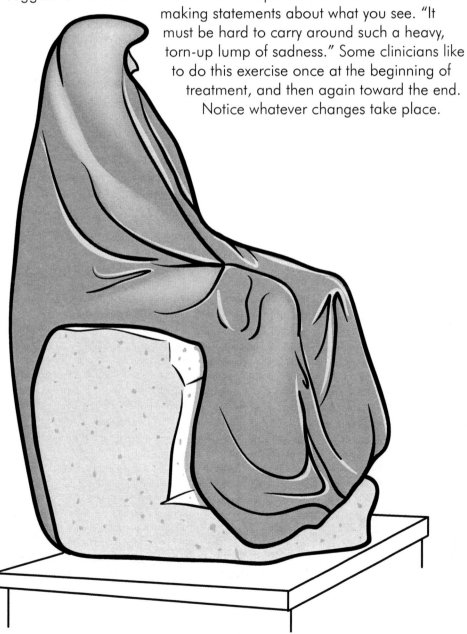

✔ **Tip:** This activity (and others using "loose" materials like fingerpaints or sand) may elicit disturbing behavior on the part of the child. It's always a judgment call: on the one hand, it brings children relief to act out events in the presence of others; on the other, children need to remain in some semblance of control. Check in with the child frequently to make sure he's okay, and calmly bring the activity to a close if he seems to be coming undone.

Baggage Check

"Boy, does he have issues… he's got a lot of baggage." How often have we heard this lament? Instead of lugging all that baggage through life, why not check it, and let a plane fly it 3,000 miles away? This simple exercise contains much of the grist of good psychotherapy. It identifies charged issues and provides a structure to work away at them.

Objective: To list and process distressing incidents in a child's life.

Materials and Preparation: Paper and pencil. A box decorated with an airplane. (This can be home-made with a shoebox and pasted-on pictures of a plane.)

Activity: Have the child make a list of bad things that have happened to him. These can range from big (sexual abuse) to small (getting saddled with taking the dog out). Put each incident on a separate strip of paper. When the child is done, put them all into the shoe box. Shake up the box, let the child reach in and grab a piece of paper, and start the discussion. Have the child work on the selected item almost every session—you'll know the topic is finished when it no longer evokes fear or shame. (Decide together when this is.) Is the topic exhausted, the paper primed for throwing away? Or should it go back to the box, safe and sound for another day?

> ✔ **Tip:** Don't force the child to discuss an item before he or she is ready. It's fine to put a topic back in the box without having talked about it at all!

T. P. Artillery

This activity seeks to link physical movement to release anger with the trigger that's causing the anger. I've heard about it done with a number of different materials—clay, squeezable balls, eggs, etc. One therapist I met recently uses wet toilet paper, providing a kind of "wink" that prevents the exercise from getting too heavy or intense.

Objective: To emotionally and physically release anger.

Materials and Preparation: Toilet paper and water. Butcher block paper and some markers. This activity works best once you have a good understanding of why the child feels angry.

Activity: Ask the child to draw the outline of the person (or thing) that she is most angry with or most afraid of. Label this drawing if you like, and tape it up on the wall. Together with the child, wet some torn-off pieces of toilet paper until they turn into mushy blobs. Now, allow the child to hurl these blobs at the representational drawing as hard as she can, saying something to the figure each time. These statements might be "I hate you because...," "You made me feel...," or, "I hope that..." You should take turns, too, drawing on your knowledge of what has happened. Yell loudly, and encourage the child to be specific and creative with her insults.

> ✔ **Tip:** You might remind the child that the figure isn't real and she isn't really hurting anyone. This can prevent feelings of guilt or fear of retaliation, and help children manage their feelings in the outside world. If the child has problems with impulse control, it can be helpful to make a point along the following lines: "It's okay to throw things at a picture of a person, but it's not ever okay to throw things at a real person."

Bouncing for Columbine

Amber Gray brought five small rubber balls to Columbine the day after the shootings. She entered a room with three girls that had been in lock-down and gave them all balls to bounce. At first, the girls bounced the balls furiously, saying they didn't know why the murders happened and how mad they were at Dylan and Eric. Amber began weaving in gentle questions. "What do you mean?" she asked at one point. "What would that look like?" she asked at another.

After a while, the girls started to bounce balls in honor of all the children who died, musing about whether all the deceased children would get to heaven. They decided that for every hundred bounces, a child would get in. "Their movements got more and more rhythmic as time passed," says Amber. "It was like a moving prayer."

By session's end, the girls opted to bounce Dylan and Eric to heaven, too.

Objective: To help feelings connected to an incident move through children's bodies and be released.

Materials: A medium-sized ball. A room where things can't get broken.

Activity: Explain to the child that sometimes kids like to bounce balls when they have strong feelings. They can bounce the ball as hard as they like, or throw it against the wall. If they want, they can say or think things about the person or situation that makes them angry. As Amber did, think about the progression of rhythm and associations of meaning as children engage in this activity.

Section 7
TAMING THE DRAGON

Traumatic events leave a litany of negative emotions in their wake, from anxiety to anger to apathy. These activities are designed to help children cope with unpleasant and self-destructive feelings, paving the way for feeling better. Intended to go hand-in-hand with those in "Expressing Feelings," these activities assist children as they regain control of their bodies and emotions. Slowly, children can begin to integrate the distress of what has happened to them.

Catalogue of Worries

Facing Fear

The Secret Life of Snakes

The Boondoggling Bog

Menacing Monster Meets His Match

Hot Ire Balloons

Catalogue of Worries

I t's comforting to imagine there's something we can do about the things we worry about—and most of the time this is true. The challenge is that in many children's lives there are worries that are serious, legitimate, and with few obvious solutions. If you sugarcoat too much, you'll lose credibility; on the other hand, if you're an intrepid problem-solver, you'll model this skill for the child.

This activity is best for the older children in our age range.

Objective: To help the child identify things that are troubling. To provide a way to remember what to do to feel better.

Materials and Preparation: Obtain ten or twenty colored index cards, and a pretty ribbon or sturdy clip.

Activity: Encourage the child to share things she worries about. List each thing separately on the front of an index card. On the back of the card, brainstorm things to do to counteract the worry—building on the child's own words and ideas whenever possible. For example, one worry might be getting picked on during the bus ride to school. Strategies to deal with this worry might include telling adults such as a teacher or the bus driver, or sitting with friends. Once you believe most of the child's worries are represented, tie up the cards with the ribbon. Decide together where to put the bundle of cards for safekeeping.

Help the child get into the habit of actively referring to these cards when problems come up. Add to the cards—both worries and solutions—over the course of your time spent together.

> ✓ **Tip:** Lots of therapists use Guatemalan "worry dolls" with children. These tiny, colorful dolls are widely available; they can also be homemade with clothespins, markers, and sparkles. According to lore, if you put these dolls under your pillow when you go to sleep, they'll "do the worrying for you, so you don't have to."

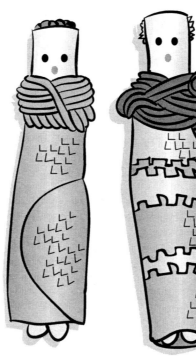

Facing Fear

"You gain strength, courage, and confidence by every experience in which you really stop to look fear in the face. You are able to say to yourself, 'I lived through this horror, I can take the next thing that comes along…' You must do the thing you think you cannot do."

—Eleanor Roosevelt

Lots of children develop particular fears and phobias after a traumatic event and invest a great deal of time and energy into avoiding reminders. Children may be terrified of the subway, of elevators, or of a particular street in their neighborhood. While these avoidance reactions usually go away with time, sometimes they become more entrenched.

Objective: To help the child overcome phobic reactions.

Materials and Preparation: This will depend on the trigger.

Activity: Find out from the child and the family what is most frightening for the child. Design an activity in which the child encounters this frightening phenomenon. Begin with imagery, pictures, or memories and proceed extremely slowly. Little by little, increase the amount of exposure giving lots of praise and encouragement. Take care not to overwhelm the child. Forcing a terrified child is doubly traumatic, as he will also feel betrayed by you.

✔ **Tip:** This is common sense but bears mentioning—children's #1 general fear is that something will happen to their parents. Any reassurance you can provide in this regard will be invaluable to the child as long as it can be provided with integrity.

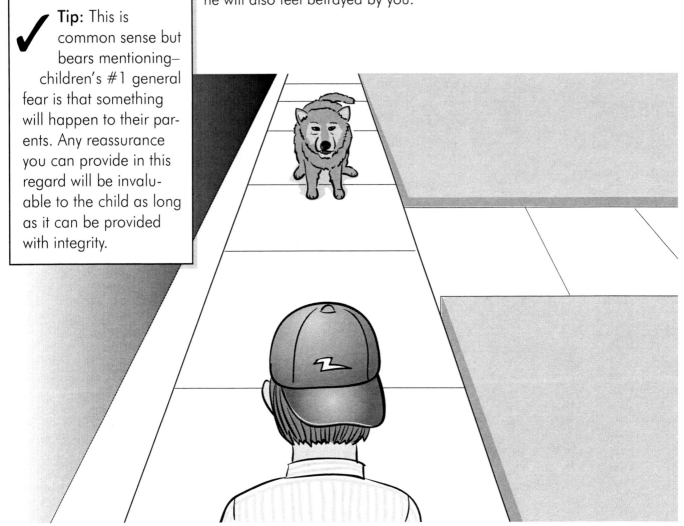

The Secret Life of Snakes

Kids gravitate toward this activity naturally when you give them clay. Be as unstructured as possible, letting this be about large rather than small motor activity. Play therapy techniques—letting scenarios evolve naturally from the materials at hand, with attention to parallels in the child's own life—are especially applicable here.

Snakes shed their skins and thus are a symbol for rebirth and regeneration. They also evoke fear; this activity presents a safe way for children to address these themes.

Objectives: To help the child master fear or aggression and gain tactile release.

Materials: A lot of Play-Doh® or clay.

Activity: Suggest making "snakes." The child will need to pound, pull, flatten, and knead the clay. Once a bunch of snakes are made, see what the child does with them! You can ask questions like "What are the snakes about to do?" or "Tell me a story about these snakes." Do the snakes try to bite each other or you? Are they poisonous rattlers or just harmless garter snakes? Whenever possible, put into words what you see going on.

Without sounding Pollyannaish, try to find out why the snakes want to bite so much (if, in fact, they're being aggressive). Are they angry? Hungry? In their natural habitat, most snakes strike only when they feel threatened; they don't go around biting everyone in sight.

> ✓ **Tip:** Who wants to go home when they could be slithering snakes? Make sure to give children plenty of warning about transitions, especially during activities that provide engrossing entry into another world. Ten minutes, then five minutes before the activity must draw to a close, let the child know this shift is approaching.

The Boondoggling Bog

This activity can be very physical with a good deal of pounding and aggressive shaping of clay, or more thoughtful as children decide which color goes with which emotion, mix suitably ugly hues, and consider the fate of figures skydiving into the panorama.

Objective: To help children cope with intolerable feelings. To externalize these feelings and create distance from them.

Materials and Preparation: Play-Doh®, an unbreakable, medium-sized bowl, and a selection of small plastic dolls that fit into the bottom of the bowl. Make peace with the fact that your Play-Doh® is about to be ruined.

Activity: Introduce the notion that sometimes when people feel down, it feels like they're at the bottom of a deep pit surrounded by terrible feelings they just can't escape. Have the child line the bowl with Play-Doh®, mixing it to create colors that show the bad feelings of a bog—these could be mustard-browns, sickly greens, or pallid, toad-belly grays.

> ✔ **Tip:** This activity offers an opportunity to discuss our own role in transcending bad moods, including that impossible uphill climb and accepting help from others.

Once the bog is complete, have the child put a figurine down there. What's it like down there? Can the doll climb out itself, or does it need help from outsiders? (Make sure both these healthy options are considered by the child.) What happens if the figurine just sits down and refuses to move? By session's end, make sure the figurine has made its way out, one way or another!

Menacing Monster Meets His Match

Facing down a monster with an adult in a well-lit room is a far cry from confronting one alone in your bedroom. Our goal here is to "lend our egos" to the child; with any luck, some of the calm and strength we exude will rub off. This activity works best with the younger children in the age range of the book.

Objective: To externalize, contain, and manage frightening feelings. To be able to conjure up benevolent forces.

Materials and Preparation: Paper and colored pens or pencils.

Activity: Have your child draw the worst, scariest and meanest monster he or she can possibly imagine. What qualities and abilities does this monster have? Now, draw a match for the monster: something more powerful than even Grendel; brainstorm together what this might be. How is this force or creature able to whip the monster into submission? What does that hapless monster look like afterwards? It's better to strive for monster management rather than extermination, since this rings more true to life.

> ✓ **Tip:** It's always good to mull over what a monster might represent in the life of the child—for example, the uncle with that head injury who goes into unpredictable rages.

PLEASE
DO NOT
FEED THE
MONSTER

Hot Ire Balloons

This ingenious activity engages children's emotional, physical and intellectual realms simultaneously. When your inner rage takes shape before your very eyes, with an invitation to whack it, sit on it, and then explode it, your state of mind inevitably becomes more buoyant!

This activity has been used successfully by a number of therapists I know; one traced it back to a workshop given by Neil Cabe.

This activity is for use with a group.

Objective: To name triggers and work through associated anger.

Materials and Preparation: Balloons to blow up. Very small strips of paper, pens or pencils, and a large space free of breakable objects.

Activity: Have children think of something that made them mad in the last week (or month, or whatever), and ask them to write it down on one of the small strips of paper. Next, have children insert the piece of paper into the balloon, which hasn't been blown up yet. This can be a little tricky. Now, have children blow ALL of their anger into the balloon, every last bit. See if they can feel the anger blowing out of them, right down to the tips of their toes.

> ✔ **Tip:** Remember, underneath anger is usually sadness and hurt.

Once all the balloons are blown up, it's time for the next step. Children should be instructed to throw their balloon in the air, and keep it in the air for a solid minute. This may involve a fair amount of running around, batting at the balloon, and tumbling into each other. Regardless of how children felt when they were blowing up their balloons, by this point they are usually giggling and having fun.

The final step is a crescendo of popping! (If you suspect children are struggling with PTSD, warn them that there will be a loud noise and allow them to leave the room if they like.) Have everybody pop their balloons by sitting on them. Children may find each other's written proclamations of anger on the floor amidst shreds of balloon. Consider having children offer solutions to each other, if the moment seems right. "So what could Harry do to feel better about...," you might ask the group.

Section 8

CHERISHING MEMORIES

Because traumatic events may include the death of a loved one, these activities support children as they grieve. The activities in this section are designed to help children reckon with loss, hold on to memories, and internalize sources of validation and strength.

It's a Wonderful Life

A Letter from Beyond

Celebrating Anniversaries

Waving Goodbye

It's a Wonderful Life

This activity can be used when someone important in the child's life has died or gone away. The idea is to create a memory book filled with treasures; ticket stubs, scrawled handwritten notes, those red-eyed Polaroids—it's strange how evocative these items can be years later. Recollections of all kinds—positive and not so positive—will be gathered, arranged, and transcribed. Memories don't have to be grand—even the most random, tiny details create the texture of a life.

This activity also can be used to help children internalize benevolent others. When the child feels anxious and alone, reassuring memories and associations can be conjured up.

Objective: To make a permanent keepsake. To demonstrate the possibility of holding on to memories and feelings associated with special people.

Materials and Preparation: A diary or album—preferably one the child likes.

Activity: Begin by affixing to the title page a photograph of the person receiving tribute. Explain to the child that together, over multiple sessions, you are going to remember as many things as you can about the person and write them down or draw them in the book. Questions to get you started include: What did the person like to do? To eat? What things did you do together? What did the person look like? What will the child miss about the person? Gather any objects associated with the person, and put these in as well. If others who knew the person can participate (and if the child is receptive), by all means have them do so.

> **✓ Tip:** Timing is tricky on this activity. It's good to do it when children's memories are fresh, but not to embark so soon that it's unduly painful.

A Letter from Beyond

I once treated a nine-year-old girl whose father was murdered in a bar. She had always been an excellent student and had warm memories of being helped with her homework by her father. After his death, she essentially went "on strike" in terms of school, refusing to complete assignments months and even years after his passing. In her mind, succeeding academically would have been a betrayal of her father, a symbolic statement that she no longer needed him. This activity strengthens children's own life-affirming impulses, while resolving some of the conflict that might prohibit healing.

Objective: To promote a child's capacity to "move on." To reinforce the bonds of caring that connect the child with this important person.

Materials and Preparation: Paper and pencil. This activity should be undertaken once you know the child pretty well.

Activity: Suggest to the child that she write a letter to herself from the deceased (or absent) person containing advice about what she should do. The letter can focus on a single issue, or can contain general advice for living—for example, addressing the question "What should I do with the rest of my life?"

Have the child imagine as fully as possible what this important person would think and say, and write these things down in letter form beginning with "Dear..." In the instance of my nine-year-old client, her "letter" contained encouragement from her (internalized) father, expressions of his love for her, assurances that he was doing well in heaven, and naturally, his wish that she be the best student she could be!

Celebrating Anniversaries

Have you ever had thoughts or dreams about a significant person gone from your life, then realized that the anniversary of their death is fast approaching? It's almost as if we have an unconscious clock that keeps track of our losses, delineating time for us in obscure ways. These patterns also apply to children; find out when during the year significant losses in their lives took place, and keep track as these dates approach.

Objective: To facilitate the mourning process over time.

Materials and Preparation: Materials will be dictated by the ritual the child selects. This activity is best done in concert with parents or other guardians.

Activity: Mention that it's been almost a year since (whoever it is) passed away, and you wonder if the child has been thinking about this person. If appropriate, have the child plan a ritual—it might be lighting a candle, looking at photographs, singing a song—or almost any other activity. Encourage the child to share thoughts and feelings throughout.

✓ **Tips:** Children grieve losses in a "staggered" fashion as they gain sophistication developmentally. Thus, anniversaries hold different meanings for children each year; it can be helpful to provide structured opportunities to process loss over time.

Waving Goodbye

This widely-used activity helps younger children cope with the loss of a beloved person or pet. Often, children have been unable to say goodbye properly since departures can be sudden and unexpected. This exercise can create some closure for the child.

I first heard about this activity from the Dougy Center, a program for grieving children in Portland, Oregon. I was lucky to visit once, and remember entire rooms dedicated to particular themes. Picture if you will a room with dozens of pillows, a room crowded with punching bags, a room with huge dollhouses and hundreds of dolls, and a room for wild, psychedelic painting—floors, windows, walls and all! Gifted therapists meet children on their own terms, and enter their world 100%!

Objective: To process loss.

Materials: Construction paper or oak tag, a popsicle stick, blunt scissors, and tape. If you like, you can use contact paper to laminate the hand afterwards as described in "Stop Right There!"

Activity: Have the child trace her hand onto the piece of paper, then cut it out. On each finger, write down what the child would like to say to the person that is gone. These can be loving, angry, or sad sentiments (just make sure they are the child's own).

Once the child's words have been written on the fingers, attach the popsicle stick with the tape. Say the person's name together, and wave good-bye.

Section 9
RESTORING BALANCE AND TRUST

These activities promote a sense of stability and benevolence in the world. Whereas "Taming the Dragon" addresses threats emanating from the inside—feeling states associated with PTSD, for example—this section helps children withstand real-life stress. Intended to fortify, center and protect, these activities encourage children to venture back into the rough-and-tumble world.

These Are a Few of My Favorite Things

Solar System of Support

Positive Mirroring

Speak Directly into the Mike

The Epicenter

Strong Mountain, Supple Tree

These Are a Few of My Favorite Things

As many of us recall, the Von Trapp children from *The Sound of Music* used this song to feel better as they were escaping Hitler through the Alps. Their mother was dead, their father was broke, and Nazis had taken up residence in their manor home. Sometimes it helps to remember our favorite things.

Objective: To provide a means of self-soothing.

Materials and Preparation: The song lyrics below.

Activity: Read and sing the original lyrics together. Then use the lyrics as a starting point to come up with the child's favorite things. Next, change the lyrics, substituting the child's own words. They don't have to rhyme, but they do have to include the child's own thoughts! Be open to whimsy. After personalizing this song, make sure to sing it through together a few times. If at all possible, both of you should memorize it.

"My Favorite Things" Lyrics

Raindrops on roses and whiskers on kittens,
Bright copper kettles and warm woolen mittens,
Brown paper packages tied up with strings,
These are a few of my favorite things...

Cream colored ponies and crisp apple strudel,
Doorbells and sleighbells and schnitzel with noodles,
Wild geese that fly with the moon on their wings,
These are a few of my favorite things...

Girls in white dresses with blue satin sashes,
Snowflakes that stay on my nose and eyelashes,
Silver white winters that melt into springs,
These are a few of my favorite things...

When the dog bites,
When the bee stings,
When I'm feeling sad,
I simply remember my favorite things,
And then I don't feel so bad.

Solar System of Support

Did you know that our sun has nine planets, the star Upsilon Andromedae has three planets, and most stars have no planets at all? Use this activity to reinforce the supportive figures in a child's life, and the plain dumb luck that leads to sparsely and densely populated constellations (small and large networks of support). Some children find themselves with a mother and a younger brother, and that's about it; other children end up with two sets of parents, a vanload of siblings, and hoards of uncles, aunts, and cousins—all cheerfully residing in the same small town.

Objective: To identify positive figures in a child's life and to instill hope.

Materials and Preparation: Pieces of white felt, cut into circles of various sizes, and one circle of yellow felt to represent the sun. A large, blue piece of posterboard and some glue. A simpler variation is to have the child draw the sun and planets on a piece of paper.

✓ **Tip:** We never know who will join our orbit as we make our way through life. It's exciting to contemplate the friends we'll meet in the future—people who'll become an important part of our lives. This can be a valuable point of discussion for children.

Activity: Ask the child to make a solar system, placing the sun (himself) in the center with various white felt circles (important people) revolving around. Suggest that the child place very supportive people closer to him, and less supportive people further away. People who are dead or absent can be included, too; like far-away stars, these figures still emit glow. Glue the sun and planets onto the posterboard in their designated spots, and label each with a black magic marker underneath. Talk about who each person is and why the child made each respective decision about placement.

YOU ARE HERE

Positive Mirroring

This activity is labor-intensive but pays off in terms of creating an object with symbolic significance. The idea is to create a mirror surrounded by photos of loved ones that the child can look into when bolstering is needed.

Objective: To internalize support from positive figures.

Materials and Preparation: Photographs, shellac or glue, and a mirror with a wide, flat wooden frame. If at all possible, involve a parent in this activity. If a real mirror is too daunting, use the format on the next page to make a collage.

Activity: Brainstorm with the child who supportive figures might be, and come up with as many as possible. Enlist the parent in retrieving photos of these figures; if none are available, consider taking quick Polaroids. Next, organize the photos around the mirror's frame, grouping them however the child thinks best. Using glue or shellac, attach photographs to the wooden frame and let it dry in between sessions.

Explain that the child can look in the mirror whenever he feels down and can then be surrounded by all the people in the world who care about him. Decide together where to put the mirror.

> ✔ **Tip:** Some children have few positive adults in their lives. In this instance, pick teachers or extended family who have taken an interest in the child—and, of course, there's always you. It only takes one caring, involved adult in a child's life to make a difference.

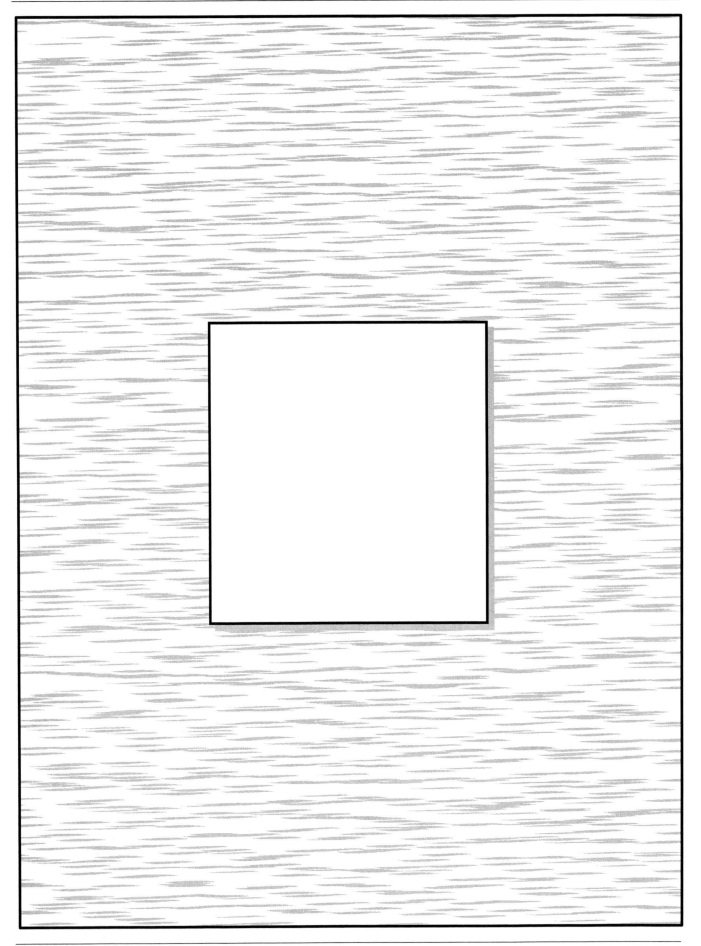

Speak Directly into the Mike

This interviewing activity entails kids talking to the important people in their lives and capturing their voices on tape. When children's environments are chaotic and in flux, having something to hold on to makes them feel more in control. Moreover, certain family members and friends may have a calming effect on the child. These feelings will then be available at a push of the "play" button.

Objective: To document and celebrate significant figures in the child's life.

Materials: A tape recorder and several cassette tapes. Make sure the recorder's microphone is of sufficient quality to pick up voices at a distance.

Activity: Children will need to do this activity on their own outside of your office. Your role is to explain it to them, get them started, and share the results. Have the child identify three or four people whom she would like to interview. Create a brief questionnaire with items such as those listed below. Between sessions, have the child schedule and conduct interviews, aiming for ten minute talks. When she returns, ask how it went and listen to the tape together.

> ✓ **Tip:** When it seems fitting, note times when the subject speaks affectionately to the child and times when the interview's content is especially interesting, unique, etc. The idea is to cultivate the child's pride in her family and sense of self.

What are some of the most vivid memories from your life?

What are some important things you've learned?

Can you tell me about family members that I never met?

What are some things you've done that you feel most proud of?

What do you remember about times we've spent together?

The Epicenter

The metaphor of an epicenter seems so fitting given our tornado-like, overscheduled lives. Even when things are hectic, a quiet and peaceful place exists internally if we can just make our way to it.

This activity is for use with a group of children.

Objective: To help children relax and center themselves.

Materials and Preparation: A soft rug or mat to sit on. If you have experience with yoga, let that wisdom come forth here!

Activity: Tell children what an epicenter is—the quiet center of a storm. Epicenters are absolutely still while everything swirls and howls around them. Together, children are going to be an epicenter for just one or two minutes. Have them sit in a circle and hold hands. (Or, if fidgeting promises to be an issue, have them rest their arms on their knees, with their palms up.) Ask them to take deep, relaxed breaths but otherwise remain absolutely still—no talking allowed. If you like, you can introduce the concept that sometimes when our bodies are quiet, we're more aware of the thoughts we're having and can take in information in purer form.

Tap a glass to begin, and tap a glass to end.

✓ **Tip:** Remember, this is hard for kids, so give lots of praise for even the smallest time spent motionless.

Strong Mountain, Supple Tree

Yoga for kids is taking off because it's fun and makes them feel better. At the same time, yoga has been used with trauma survivors of all ages with remarkable results. To a certain extent, trauma is "stored" in the physical body and can be inaccessible through talking cures. The spiritual tenets underlying yoga can also bring peace and meaning in the face of horror.

Objective: To learn about the practice of yoga; to gain strength, flexibility, and balance.

Materials and Preparation: A mat and comfortable clothes.

Activity: Shake out the arms and legs, loosening up before beginning. The first pose will be the mountain pose. Have the child stand with the insides of her feet together, feeling her feet spread and connect to the floor. Tighten the leg muscles, tuck in the posterior, let arms relax by the sides and look straight ahead. "Picture a spot between your eyebrows, and slowly trace a line from your forehead all the way to the ground," you might say. Through this exercise, children direct their attention inward. Energy stays focused—ceasing to scatter—as "mountains" become ever more still.

Once the child has got "Mountain" down, give "Tree" a try. Begin from the child's sturdy Mountain pose. Then, have her lift one knee up so it's parallel to the ground, bring it straight out to the side, and tuck the top of her foot on the inside of her upper leg. As a final touch, the child can place the palms of her hands together and touch her thumbs to her chest. Hold this pose for ten seconds or so. Repeat, using the other leg.

✓ **Tip:** It's less important to get the poses technically correct than it is to reinforce the metaphors of strength, flexibility, and balance. Have the child truly feel what it is to "be" a mountain and a tree, closing her eyes and breathing deeply as she calls up these images. Remember, branches get buffeted around by strong winds but bend instead of breaking, and mountains endure over milleniums!

Section 10
I CAN FEEL GOOD

These activities address children's self-esteem. Especially in cases of abuse and neglect, children feel devalued by others and thus never learn to nurture themselves. By practicing constructive internal talk, recognizing strengths, and gaining perspective about what transpired, children can begin to appreciate their talents and goodness.

Therefore I Am

Friend in Training

100 Great Things about Me

Cascade of Excellence

A Day in the Life of Me

Therefore I Am

Children who have known abuse or neglect are prone to negative feelings about themselves–"ugly," "dumb," or "worthless." Lacking the input of admiring adults, a devaluing inner soundtrack can haunt children for much of their lives. Therapists need to teach children to talk to themselves more positively. Don't be afraid to give the child compliments. Your approving voice will come into his mind, chasing away dark ruminations.

Objective: To help children make connections between their thoughts and feelings.

Materials: Refer to the picture on the following page. This boy has spilled his lunch tray in front of everyone.

Activity: Discuss the concept of positive and negative self-talk. Brainstorm the things the boy could say to himself that would make him feel bad ("That was stupid," for example, or "I'm so clumsy.") Next, think of examples of thoughts that could leave him feeling better ("It was just an accident," or "Last week Amelia spilled hers, too.") Write down these statements in the thought bubbles that are part of the picture.

Friend in Training

When something bad happens to someone, it can be hard to know the right thing to say. Even grown-ups sometimes pop out with things that actually make everyone feel worse than they did before. It's important to remember that when this happens, it's usually because the person just doesn't know what to do or is feeling bad themselves.

Objective: To improve social skills and recognize hurtful statements when they are made by others.

Activity: Read the statements on the back of this page, and decide whether each is helpful or hurtful. Draw a string between each balloon and who you think might have made the statement enclosed in the balloon. (The good friend is on the left, the needs-a-crash-course-in-friendship candidate is on the right.)

> ✔ **Tip:** Sometimes it's hard to tell whether a comment is helpful or hurtful! In these cases, discuss with the child what makes the comment seem one way or another.

100 Great Things about Me

One hundred seems like a huge number to kids, and 100 positive attributes about themselves is practically inconceivable! Near the beginning of your time working together, make a bet that by the time you finish, you'll have come up with "100 Great Things" about the child.

Objective: To build self-esteem. To feel known and appreciated.

Materials: Some therapists like to write these on an inexpensive lampshade. When completed, the child can bring it home and find a special place for it. His qualities will be illuminated each time he turns on the lamp! You can also make a T-shirt advertising the child's great qualities, to be worn "as needed." Writing on humble sheets of paper also works just fine.

Activity: Together with the child, explain the goal and begin to brainstorm good qualities covering all categories—home, family, school, sports, etc. You'll generate an initial list, which you can add to as you get to know the child better. You might spontaneously write on the list during a session focusing on something else entirely! Feel free to throw in some silly ones to lighten the tone and the task. Whatever you do, don't forget about this challenge and leave it undone.

> ✔ **Tip:** Catch children being good, and notice specific things about them that they might not notice themselves. The more subtle and well-observed your comments are, the more known your child will feel.

Cascade of Excellence

This activity is related to the previous one, and is only possible when you're working with a group of children. It's best undertaken when children have had a chance to get to know each other.

This activity is for use with a group.

Objective: To practice giving and receiving praise.

Materials: Paper and pencil.

Activity: Have children sit together in a circle, and explain that they're about to do something that will help them get to know themselves and each other a little better. Have a piece of paper for each child with their name written at the top. Pass each piece of paper around the circle with this instruction: each child must write one positive word or thought about the child whose name is at the top. Have them start at the bottom of the page and work their way up. Naturally, nothing rude or insulting is allowed!

Each time a word is added, fold the paper up so children are unable to see what previous children have written. At the end of the exercise, each child may open up his or her paper and read out loud the affirmations they find there. You might ask children if anything written was surprising to them or if there were any patterns in what they heard.

> ✓ **Tip:** Don't use this exercise if children lack control to follow instructions properly.

A Day in the Life of Me!

This activity is based on the work of Project Image, a Boston-based initiative that teaches urban teens to document their lives through photography. For groups who might feel ostracized by society—homeless people, for example—this approach is especially powerful. Children receive the message that their lives are important and gain tools to tell their own stories in their own way.

Objective: To honor the routines and people in your everyday life and build self-esteem.

Materials and Preparation: A disposable camera and sufficient funds to develop the film.

Activity: Explain to the child that together you will pick one day, and the child will photograph all the typical events of that day. These might include getting ready for school, fighting over the bathroom, doing last minute homework on the bus, etc. Discuss with the child what these key moments might be, leaving plenty of room for improvisation and spontaneity. Once the photos are developed, assist the child in assembling them into a scrapbook. What does each photograph say about how the child was feeling at that time?

Tip: Structure and routine are especially important to think about after a traumatic event. This activity helps reinforce "everydayness" so it becomes embedded in the back of the child's mind.

HEROES

Heroes overcome difficult circumstances to reach goals they never dreamed possible. These activities reinforce children's growing sense of self-efficacy and power, while acknowledging that some negative feelings and scenarios never quite go away. Here, we celebrate the courage necessary for emotional growth, and the arc of the hero's journey from despair to a sense of optimism and well-being.

Happily Ever After

On Top of the World

Building Bridges

The River Sticks

Sanctity of Sadness

Wings of a Butterfly

Happily Ever After

One of the salient aspects of trauma is powerlessness. I think of the following exercise as less of an activity than a technique—one long used by play therapists in their work with vulnerable children.

Done clumsily, this technique will feel like an imposition. Done with subtlety and imagination, new dynamics weave seamlessly into the child's play and shake loose "stuck" emotions and themes. The trick is to introduce a different, "better" ending at just the right moment.

Objective: To promote feelings of mastery and optimism.

Materials and Preparation: A group of dolls, puppets, or stuffed animals, used as "actors" similar to those involved in the traumatic event. Imagine a scenario that is close to—but doesn't exactly duplicate—the traumatic event experienced by the child. Better yet, introduce this technique when the child is already playing out the scenario spontaneously.

Activity: Using an example such as a dam breaking, the therapist could say something along these lines: "Let's pretend there was a flood, and some people were caught in the water and didn't know how to swim. I'll be the father and you be the little boy. But this time, you have special powers and can make the story end however you want it to. Okay, where should I be first…"

✓ **Tip:** Child therapists become adept at "playing a part" which is actually the child's creation. They ask questions such as, "Okay, now what should the father do?" and supply animated dialogue consistent with what the child has in mind. Thus, the child is actually the motivating force for all the characters in a drama.

On Top of the World

T his activity draws on the principles of sand tray therapy, but uses materials that are convenient and help children stay in better control emotionally. The idea is to create a metaphorical world through which the child can portray aspects of his or her own psychological reality.

Objective: To play out preoccupations and conflicts. To promote mastery. To envision "better" endings.

Materials and Preparation: A large piece of white cardboard (about twenty inches by thirty inches), and a whole potpourri of animals, people, and objects. These could include: little houses, blocks, holiday decorations, dolls roughly representative of the child's family, cotton for snow, pens and markers, ribbons, cars, dinosaurs, empty aspirin bottles, etc. Offbeat items as well as items with relevance to the child's life are good.

Activity: Place the cardboard on the floor; this is the backdrop for the world the child is about to create. Have the materials handy. Make a statement along these lines to the child: "Tell me a story. This is your world, and you can make up any story you want in this world." Don't direct the child's activity. Whatever spontaneously emerges will likely be related to issues in the child's life.

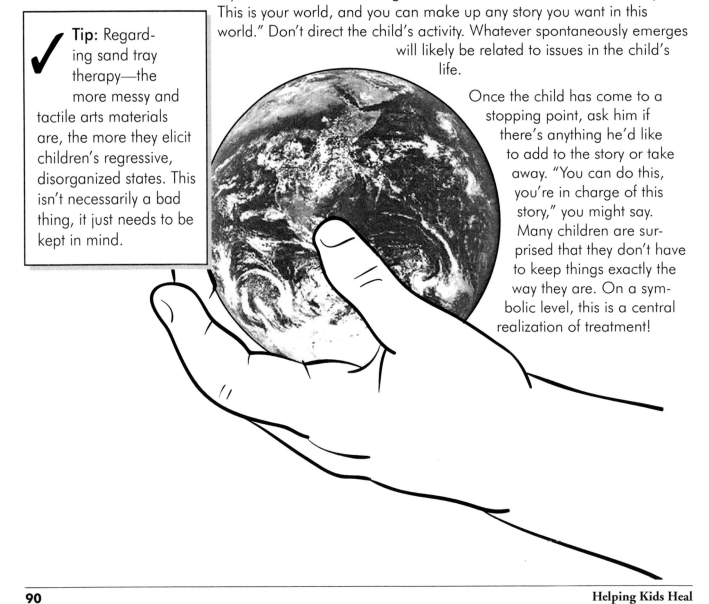

✓ **Tip:** Regarding sand tray therapy—the more messy and tactile arts materials are, the more they elicit children's regressive, disorganized states. This isn't necessarily a bad thing, it just needs to be kept in mind.

Once the child has come to a stopping point, ask him if there's anything he'd like to add to the story or take away. "You can do this, you're in charge of this story," you might say. Many children are surprised that they don't have to keep things exactly the way they are. On a symbolic level, this is a central realization of treatment!

Building Bridges

Τhis is a cooperative activity for a group of children, good for discussing whatever emotional "journey" is at hand. I heard about it from a Child Life specialist who used it in her work with children and teens with terminal illness. Noncompetitive activities and games are especially valuable for fragile children.

This activity is for use with a group.

Objective: To work together toward a common goal. To provide a metaphor for emotional growth and to measure children's perception of their progress.

Materials and Preparation: All kinds of arts and crafts materials are needed, from cardboard to pipe cleaners, colored paper and pens of all sorts, paper towel tubes, styrofoam cups and sheets of foam-core, posterboard, collage materials, etc. You'll also need little figurines, perhaps the same ones as used in Boondoggling Bog.

Activity: Instruct children to work together to build a bridge out of the materials at hand. Tell them that everyone has to have input and a role; beyond that, they can create the bridge however they like. Once the form is completed, decide together what the bridge represents. Have children place a figurine (themselves) somewhere on the bridge. Consider discussing why each child placed his or her figure where they did, and what they can all do to successfully get across to the other side.

✔ **Tip:** Carefully watch for "red flags" as children place their figures. For example, one depressed boy placed his proxy on the bridge in the path of oncoming traffic.

The River Sticks

This is another activity from Amber Gray, the Colorado-based therapist who works with refugee children around the world. The activity used to be called "Minefield," but Amber renamed it because for many children this reference hit too close to home. In this game, "peanut butter" becomes a metaphor for those viscous hazards of life we just can't escape!

This activity is for use with a group of children.

Objective: To exercise children's communication, teamwork, and problem-solving skills, and to build strength and coordination. To master a "scary" situation with no real danger.

Materials and Preparation: Five or six blocks of wood, stones, or mats. At the start of the game, these will all be on one side of the "river," in a pile. (This is important—the blocks are not already in formation, creating steps across the river. Children need to position the blocks as they go.) Determine the width of the river based on the children's age and abilities—it should be about twenty or thirty feet wide. Describe the scenario: children are walking along together in the woods, and they come upon a huge river of hot, sticky peanut butter that they must cross. Everyone in the team must make it across safely!

Activity: Start with the children on one side of the "river," having recently stumbled upon this gooey predicament. Review the ground rules: a block must have a child on it at all times; no more than one child can be on a block at any one time; and if any part of a child's body touches the river, they all have to start again. Give them a time limit (say, ten minutes) and their blocks, and let the fording begin.

Sanctity of Sadness

A friend of mine went to a conference recently and "made a house for her grief," one of the most moving activities she's ever done. Neither of us relishes doing experiential activities among perfect strangers, but she entered her own little world and completely lost herself. She said it was like an inner voice took over and gave her definitive instructions. For instance, she "had" to make her house three-dimensional, give it a door, and cover it with silver glitter.

In some ways, this activity is about making peace with the pain in one's life, and acknowledging how fundamentally it can shape us. My friend said she used decorative glitter because in the final analysis, her grief gave her something she valued.

Children can do this activity singly or in groups.

Objective: To learn about and process grief.

Materials and Preparation: This activity requires a variety of arts and crafts materials, whatever is at hand. Useful are colored construction paper, materials of different textures, glitter, pipe cleaners, markers, pom-poms, glue, popsicle sticks, tape, etc.

Activity: The directions for this activity are very simple: "Make a house for your grief." Some children will simply draw an outline of a house on a piece of paper with black magic marker; others may have different rooms representing the things that make them sad. One may make a castle, a well-fortified receptacle for their feelings, while another might fashion a crude cloth tent with swinging flaps.

> ✓ **Tip:** When giving directions for this activity, it's important not to say too much. That way, children will interpret the challenge however they see fit.

Wings of a Butterfly

This activity was provided by Deborah Vilas, who used it in a therapeutic classroom for severely abused children. Deborah relied on this activity during times of transition—for example, when a class was graduating—but it demarcates emotional growth of all kinds. The idea of a cocoon—going inward to a protected place before emerging transformed—is a natural metaphor for therapy.

This activity is best for the younger children in our age range, and can be part of a whole butterfly-focused curriculum. It generally works best with groups of children.

Objective: To help children begin anew.

Materials and Preparation: The book *The Very Hungry Caterpillar*. Cloth laundry bags—one for each child. Pieces of colorful felt (about 8" by 10") in the shape of wings.

Activity: Read *The Very Hungry Caterpillar* together, and make sure children have an understanding of the whole process of caterpillars turning into butterflies. Talk about whatever links there are to children's lives: for example, "Now you're finishing therapy, and we're going to say good-bye, and you'll fly into the world feeling stronger and shinier than you were before…" or something along these lines. Be theatrical. These little caterpillars are about to turn into butterflies!

Have children crawl into their laundry bags with their felt wings. Let them know it's okay to stay in there until they feel ready to come out—this may be thirty seconds or thirty minutes. (Deborah remembers tiny voices intoning, "I'm still not ready…") Whenever the urge strikes them, children may emerge out of their cocoons and "fly" around the room fluttering their felt butterfly wings.

Section 12
WISHES AND DREAMS

"Trauma is a disorder of the imagination," says one expert, referring to the tendency to get "stuck" and visualize solely what one has experienced. These activities foster children's creative and imaginative life, including the ability to contemplate fundamentally different futures. We end with activities about making dreams come true.

Dream Catcher

Home, Home on the Range

Heart's Desire

Poetry to the Rescue

Outta Here!

Wonders of the World

Dream Catcher

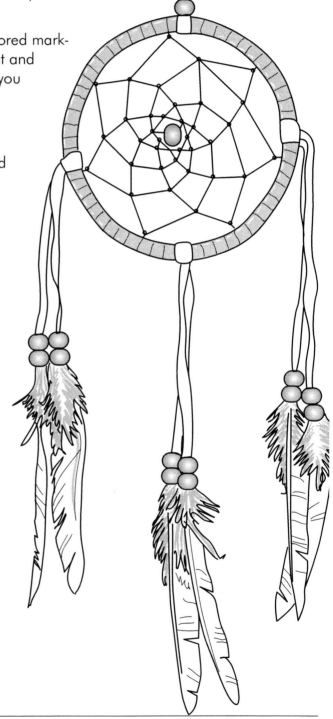

With all due respect to the randomness of brain neurochemistry, dreams contain powerful messages about our fondest wishes and fears. Children and adults alike may have nightmares after a traumatic event, and this activity can promote coping. I include two variations here, one to capture good dreams and one to blow away bad.

Objective: To learn about the content of a child's dreams, and to reinforce positive memories and fantasies.

Materials and Preparation: Some paper plates, colored markers, glue and two feet of ribbon. Feathers, glitter, paint and the like are also great to use. For the second activity, you should have vividly colored (including dark, ominous colors) sands and a large piece of cardboard.

Activity: Explain to the child that American Indians believed that you could "catch" dreams as they floated up to the sky with round decorated nets hanging over your bed. Together, you can make a special kind of dream catcher, one that catches the good dreams and lets others fly away.

Ask the child about their best dream. This could be a recent good dream, or their most wonderful dream ever. Now, have the child draw a bold picture of their good dream on the front of a paper plate. Make a small hole in the top of the plate using a pen or scissors (you'll have to help with this) and tie one end of the ribbon to it. The child can tie the dream catcher up in his or her bedroom window.

For Part 2 of this activity, we bid the American Indians farewell and visit the Aborigines. This Australian people made images of their dreams with colored sands—creating the feeling of the dream rather than an illustration. When they were finished, they blew the dreams away into the wind. What a way to handle a nightmare! Guide the child through this process, using a "bad" dream as above and the cardboard or a piece of cloth to protect your office.

Home, Home on the Range

This activity is great for having children express in a positive way what they would like to be different in their lives. Therapists can think about the degree of discrepancy between children's ideal vision of life and what their lives are actually like. Once we really allow ourselves mourning and disappointment, we're somehow freed up to work towards our vision of perfection.

This activity can be done with a single child or with a small group of children.

Objective: To acknowledge children's wishes and dreams.

Materials: Large butcher block paper and colored markers. Tape a large piece of paper onto the wall.

Activity: Ask the child to draw a picture of his or her perfect house, the one they wished they lived in. Get the child to put in as many details as possible, and discuss what parts are the same and which are different from the house he or she currently lives in.

✔ **Tip:** For a group of kids, a fun variation is to have everyone do this activity—drawing a slew of ideal homes—and then put these renditions up together to create an ideal neighborhood.

Make sure you have a good understanding of each element the child puts in—sometimes a seemingly random squiggle provides crucial insight into that child's concerns.

Heart's Desire

This activity is based on drama therapy and was contributed by Sara McMullian. She used it with children in an inpatient psychiatric hospital and found it especially effective for children who have difficulty talking about their feelings.

Sara remembers a treatment breakthrough with a particular child. This eleven-year-old boy was plagued by feelings of responsibility for his family's dysfunction, was clinically depressed, and had been cutting himself. During this exercise, he pantomimed getting out of a prison of his own making.

This activity is for use with a group of children.

Objective: To get in touch with one's wants and needs, while maintaining privacy.

Materials and Preparation: A space large enough for the group to sit and move around in comfortably. Have children arrange themselves into a circle.

Activity: The concept is this: in the center of the circle is an invisible box of any size or shape. Inside is "what each child needs, or their heart's desire." Each child decides for him or herself what this is. During their turns, the children go to the center of the circle, pantomime opening the lid of the box, and encounter/hold/interact with whatever they imagine is inside. Once the box is open, children may do whatever they like with what they find there—put it back, for example, or put it in their pocket. Sara says one child found something like "fairy dust" and gave a little bit to each child present.

> ✔ **Tip:** Unlike charades, the object is not to guess what each child is doing, only to respectfully witness their actions.

Poetry to the Rescue

C reative writing is a great way to help children work through difficult emotions. One of the great things about poetry is that it takes something that might be ugly—shaky, scary feelings, for example—and gives it a certain stark beauty. This activity is applicable for older children—and even so, they may still need help!

Objective: To understand and express feelings. To use creative writing to transcend circumstances.

Materials and Preparation: This activity will only be possible if the child is familiar with poetry. Lay some groundwork by reading poetry together and discussing how there are words of all kinds to express feelings. I've included a poem by my eight-year-old niece Louisa as an example.

Activity: Encourage the child to write a poem about a time that she was afraid of something and then was able to overcome it. The poem doesn't have to rhyme and can be either short or long. Ideally, the poem will describe what she was afraid of and why, exactly what led to the change, and what led to feeling okay about the problem. Once the poem is done, read it out loud.

That Storm

That storm,
That storm,
It scares me,
The thunder,
The lightning,
The rain.
The trees are whipping in the wind,
The wind is so strong,
The sound is so scary.
It makes me so wary.
It scares me much more,
But I listen much harder,
Deep under my covers
I notice
The storm sounds so friendly,
I'm deep in my book,
My brothers are napping,
It's quiet,
Just look.

By Louisa Wilde Carman, 2002

Outta Here!

By the time Manny Ramirez was a teenager, he knew he wanted to be a major league baseball player more than anything. He got up at 4:30 a.m., fastened an old tire to a rope around his waist, and ran up and down the hills of Washington Heights. Five years later, Manny had his first major league game at Yankee Stadium. As friends and relatives screamed ecstatically, Manny hit two home runs and a double—those years of sweat and exertion paid off in spades!

Kids often don't realize how much hard work lies behind success. Help children identify what they'd like to be good at, and figure out steps they can take right now to move toward that goal.

Objective: To gain a realistic sense of what it takes to succeed. To build purpose in life.

Materials and Preparation: The questionnaire found on the following page and pen or pencil.

Activity: Together with the child, discuss each question along the "road" and fill in the blanks.

When do you have the most fun? _____

_____

_____

What is your best talent? _____

_____

_____

When you're eighteen, what do you hope to be doing? _____

_____

_____

What about at age twenty-eight, and thirty-eight? _____

_____

_____

Do you know anyone who is doing these things? _____

_____

_____

If so, how did they do it? _____

_____

_____

What can you do—right now—to have the kind of life you want later on? _____

_____

_____

_____

Wonders of the World

This is a signature activity from storyteller Laura Simms, who tells marvelous tales from around the world. Laura's intuitive, soulful style helps children transcend pain and loss and encourages them to embrace all aspects of themselves. Her resource book *Becoming the World* (created for the organization Comfort for Kids) is referenced at the back of this volume.

Objective: To encourage children to imagine all the delights of the future.

Materials and Preparation: Butcher block paper, large enough so the outline of the child will fit. Colored markers and paints.

Activity: Have the child lie down on the paper, and draw his or her outline. Next, guide the child to answer the questions below, referring to the future in a general, wide-open sense—the future could be tomorrow, or it could be fifty years from now. Next, have the child place "answers" (drawings, symbols, and words) next to the appropriate area within the outline; for example, the first set of drawings should be placed next to the eyes.

Draw and write what you would like your eyes to see (in the future).

Draw and write where you would like your feet to take you.

Draw and write what you would like to eat.

Draw and write what you would like to hear or listen to.

Draw and write what you would like your hands to make.

GROWING AND GIVING BACK

These activities cultivate children's compassion and empathy. After a traumatic event, survivors must consciously choose to break the cycle; without active support, hurtful attitudes may be perpetuated. For many children, helping others is healing in and of itself.

The Giant Who Had No Heart

You're a Shining Star

Secret Santa

Guru of the Future

Lights! Camera! Action!

Inside a Whale's Stomach

Zoom into Action

The Giant Who Had No Heart

This activity is also from storyteller Laura Simms. During work with orphans in Romania, she noticed that these children seemed to be "hiding their hearts." They'd lived through so much violence and disappointment that they were tough inside and out.

Laura usually tells a story (in this instance, "The Giant Who Had No Heart" in the volume *Becoming the World*) and then engages children in activities. This activity works in conjunction with the story or on its own.

Objective: To help children regain an inner feeling of goodness.

Materials and Preparation: Large sheets of papers and colored pencils, crayons or markers. Begin this activity by making a statement along the following lines—that sometimes children feel like they have to hide their hearts to keep them safe.

Activity: In this activity, the child will create a map containing an entire landscape—including mountains, streams, rocks, wild animals, etc. You can explicitly talk about things that could hurt hearts (brambles, spears, an ice age, etc.) and the child may locate these where they belong on the map. Next, the child should decide where his heart should reside to be hidden and safely guarded. Discuss with the child how he would know it was safe for the heart to emerge. Would anything have to change in the tableau?

> ✔ **Tip:** This activity is really about understanding the connection between the things that have happened to us and how we feel and act. For instance, "mean" people have often known only cruelty.

You're a Shining Star

No matter how obstreperous the child, he must have done one nice thing for someone at some point in time. The idea is to capture and affirm this moment and have it become part of the child's conscious identity. When a child sees him or herself as, in part, someone who does kind things, only good can come of it. This is more likely when adults notice good deeds and celebrate them!

Objective: To reinforce positive self-image and prosocial behavior.

Materials and Preparation: Some paper and lots of glitter and stickers of gold stars.

Activity: Together with the child, remember one time the child did a good deed. It could be small and simple, such as opening a door for a silver-haired lady on crutches or moving a ladybug on the sidewalk out of harm's way. Write the story of this good deed with as many details as possible. How did it feel to do this deed, and how does the child imagine the recipient felt? When you're done writing, have children decorate the edges of the paper with glitter and stars. Encourage the child to share with you similar stories as they occur. Soon, you'll have a whole library of virtue.

✔ **Tip:** Children could feel pressured by this activity, and tempted to make something up to save face. If you suspect the potential for this reaction, either save the activity for later or make sure you yourself have observed something about the child that qualifies as a good deed. At all costs, avoid making the child feel ashamed.

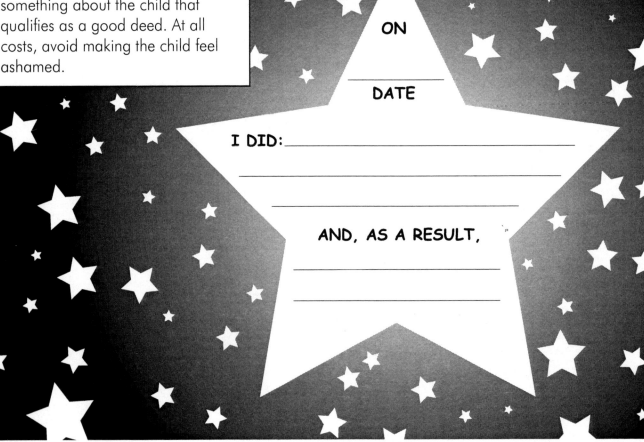

ON

_____

DATE

I DID:_____

_____

_____

AND, AS A RESULT,

_____

_____

Secret Santa

We really know we've been successful with our kids when they do kind things for others without looking for credit or reward! If we could get more citizens thinking along these lines, imagine the amount of money we'd save in taxes as people no longer dropped fast-food wrappers in the street, submitted phony insurance claims, or allowed factories to spew toxins into lakes.

Objective: To reinforce the benefit of generosity and consideration for others.

Materials and Preparation: Depends on the activity selected.

Activity: Together with the child, plot a good deed that the child will do on the Q. T. before your next session together. Be enthusiastic. Next time you see her, ask how it went, how she felt, and (if it's not overdoing it) how she imagined the recipient felt. The success of this activity really hinges on discussion and on the child's respect for, and bond with, you. If the important figures in this child's life value this perspective and way of being, it's likely the child will as well.

✔ **Tip:** It can be valuable to share what it feels like to be the recipient of a good deed. Once I was buying a necklace and the storeowner asked me what I did. I told her I managed Comfort for Kids, a Mercy Corps program that does trauma education trainings. She got very excited about the project and was concerned about how New York City's children were faring. When I got home, I found she had put an extra necklace into my bag—one even more beautiful than the one I'd selected!

Guru of the Future

The United States has seen an explosion in self-help books over the last decade, and right now it's a multibillion dollar industry. This tells us a few things: people like to try to feel better, and people like to help each other feel better.

Indirectly, this activity is a way that the therapist can show confidence in the child. It's also a way of reversing the stigma that children sometimes feel when they're in treatment. They have ideas to offer, too! This activity can be done towards the end of treatment to highlight what the child has learned.

Objective: To draw on the child's own knowledge about feeling better.

Materials: Folded-over white or lined pieces of paper to make a book. Pens or markers for the text.

✓ **Tip:** Keep in mind that the advice given by the child can provide a window into what he or she needs from others.

Activity: Explain to the child about self-help books—what they are, what they do. If you have any in your office, you can point them out and riffle through the good parts. Suggest to the child that you make a self-help book together that has recommendations for children who might be feeling sad or down. If a friend were in a bad mood, what would she tell him to cheer him up? This book can be short—a few pithy thoughts can go a long way! Make sure to use the child's own words, and don't worry about grammar or punctuation.

you are o.k. try to smile be happy

Lights! Camera! Action!

At Loews Movie Theaters, homemade PSAs shot on grainy film remind audiences to keep quiet and enjoy the show. Lights! Camera! Action! builds on this idea, and is more high-tech than the typical activity in these pages.

This activity is for use with a group of children.

Objective: To empower children to improve their own and other people's lives.

Materials: A digital video camera and a system for viewing and possibly editing. A well-lit area to serve as a stage. Not necessary but fun: a director's chair, a bullhorn, costumes, etc.

Activity: Suggest to children that they make a commercial to convince people to do something good in the world. First, children will have to come to a consensus about a community, peer, or environmental problem. They will then need to create a small skit, complete with lines, stage directions, and a role for every child.

Luckily, these skits can be short, simple and improvised! For example, a commercial addressing littering could have a child sitting in a flower garden. Actors could walk by and throw "litter" (clean, crumpled paper) around him until he is buried. A commercial about kids wanting to spend more time with their parents could have a child trying to talk to her mom who keeps rushing—frantic and wild-eyed—on to the next errand.

 **Tip:** Community Access TV stations often run projects like this.

Inside a Whale's Stomach

Have you read the 2003 Pew Oceans Commission report or taken a look at the website for disappearing species (www.massextinction.net)? In my personal opinion, every person who works with children should actively cultivate respect for the natural world. As we come full circle in our healing, it's our responsibility to reach out to others and, ultimately, put their well-being on par with our own.

I learned about this activity from HEART, a New York City-based group that provides compassion-based curriculums for schoolteachers. It works best with a group of children.

Objective: To raise awareness of the impact of our actions.

Materials: One plastic gallon jug (and part of another), 35 feet of nylon rope, one large garbage bag, a five-pound hunk of rubber, another big hunk of partially dissolved rubber, and ten small plastic items including cups, bags, utensils, bottles, etc. (I know, finding hunks of rubber is a tall order. Perhaps pieces of old tires, or galoshes...) Place all of these in a bag.

Activity: Dump the contents of the bag out, and ask the children what all the items have in common. After children have exhausted their guesses, tell them that all these objects were found in the stomach of a whale washed up on a beach in North Carolina. Lead a discussion that includes questions about how the things got into the ocean in the first place and if there's anything we can do to improve the situation.

✓ **Tip:** Use common sense and don't use this activity with children that already feel overwhelmed or guilt-ridden. If you initiate an activity like this one, make sure the children are truly ready for it and that there's something tangible they can do to help.

Zoom into Action

Studies show over and over again that children who volunteer in their communities are more engaged with the world, more empathic, and more likely to become good citizens. Some people worry that exposure to social problems will be disturbing to children; in fact, the opposite is true. True damage is done when children discover that these things are happening and the adults in their lives either don't know or don't seem to care.

This activity is based on Zoom into Action, a campaign from the PBS series ZOOM that motivates children to make a difference in their communities. Recently, Thirteen/WNET in New York put some of these enterprising, fabulous kids on TV. On the following page are some of the things they said. Learn more about them and other "zoomers" at http://www.thirteen.org/kids/zoom/zoomlight.html

Objective: To build children's self-esteem and compassion.

Materials and Preparation: The profile on the back of this page and the accompanying worksheet.

Activity: Talk over the profile on the next page. If you feel the child you're working with is interested and ready, take the next step! Talk about opportunities to volunteer that are available in your community and appeal to the child. (Be realistic—for example, if the child doesn't have anyone to help with logistics, take this into account.) Together, fill in the blank worksheet.

Lakita, Ashley, and Milan of M.S. 180, Daniel Hale Truman School in the Bronx

How I'm volunteering: We participated in the Cancer Walk.

How often I volunteer: We are always working on new projects.

Here's how I got the idea: Our teacher was diagnosed with breast cancer and we felt so hopeless. Then Ashley saw an ad for the Cancer Walk in the bank and we knew this was a way to help all women with this disease.

These are the steps I took: 1. We asked our principal for help. 2. We raised $700 in just three days. 3. We made T-shirts to wear for the Cancer Walk. 4. We had a great time participating in the walk.

One of the coolest things that happened while I volunteered: Our teacher smiled so much because she found hope and courage among the faces of the many cancer survivors we met.

Here are some results: We raised $700 for the American Cancer Society. We spent quality time with a very special mentor and friend. We completed a 5-mile race! From people reading our T-shirts, we were able to share our teacher's story.

Volunteer Questionnaire

What cause would you like to volunteer for?

_____

_____

How often would you like to volunteer?

_____

_____

How did you get this idea?

_____

_____

What steps can you take to volunteer?

_____

_____

What's one of the coolest things you'd like to have happen?

_____

_____

What results would you like to see?

_____

_____

Bibliography

Books for Children

Something Bad Happened: A Series of Six Creative Books for Healing from Post-Traumatic Stress, by Deborah Whiting Alexander. The Bureau For At-Risk Youth, (1992).

Why did it Happen? by Janice Cohn. William Morrow (1994).

A Terrible Thing Happened, by Margaret Holmes. Magination (2000).

Brave Bart, by Caroline Sheppard. The Institute for Trauma and Loss in Children (1998).

No More Secrets for Me, by Oralee Wachter. Little Brown & Company (2002).

The Very Hungry Caterpillar, by Eric Carle. Putnam Publishing Group, (1983).

Resources for Therapists

35 Ways to Help a Grieving Child, The Dougy Center.

Treating Traumatized Children: New Insights and Creative Interventions, by Beverly James. Simon & Schuster (1990).

Trauma in the Lives of Children: Crisis and Stress Management Techniques for Counselors, Teachers, and Other Professionals, by Kendall Johnson. Hunter House (2002).

101 Favorite Play Therapy Techniques, by Heidi G. Kaduson and Charles Schaefer (Editors). Volumes I, II, and III. Jason Aronson (1997, 2001, 2003).

Children and Trauma: A Guide for Parents and Professionals, by Cynthia Monahon. Jossey-Bass (1997).

Death in the School Community, by Martha Oates. American Counseling Association (1993).

Too Scared to Cry, by Lenore Terr. Basic Books (1992).

Play Therapy with Children in Crisis, by Nancy Boyd Webb. Guilford Publications (1999).

Becoming the World, by Laura Simms. Mercy Corps (2003). www.laurasimms.com.

A Word About Our Contributors

In addition to activities originating from my own clinical practice and the work of the Comfort for Kids program, this volume contains inspired ideas from New York City psychotherapists (and diverse others) who work with traumatized children. As we all know, "pearls of wisdom" are passed from colleague to colleague, from supervisor to supervisee, and from the field into the literature and back again. Some of those I spoke with took pains to say that they didn't invent the activity in question, and directed me to the relevant book or co-worker (or professor or seminar or article!) if they remembered it. Those most frequently mentioned are listed in the Resources for Therapists section on page 115. What we can all attest to is this: collectively, we have used this unique set of activities with rich success, helping countless kids move step by step toward recovery. On behalf of myself and The Bureau for At-Risk Youth, I want to thank the wonderful advocates for children listed below, as well as the clients and authors whose teachings enhance all of our work.

Generously providing time, knowledge, and enthusiasm on behalf of this project are:

Allison Avery	Pilar Olivo
Karen Bernstein	Jude Ornstein
Joe Connor	Thao Pham
Tricia Cox	Gemelyn Philogene
Barbara Golby	Clarissa Potter
Amber Gray	Constance Powers
Adrienne Haskell	Cathy Ratcliff
Keith Hefner	Laura Simms
Lucinda Hotchkiss	Farah Tanai
Marian Tan Johnson	Joanne Treistman
Aaron Jungels	Deborah Vilas
Rachelle Kammer	Karline Volcy
Sara McMullian	Joyce Weiss